STEEL RAILS ACROSS AMERICA

The drama of railroading in spectacular photos

Gary W. Dolzall

and

Mike Danneman

LEFT: As the sun sets over the distant Rockies, shining steel rails
point the way for a Burlington Northern freight near Sedalia on Colorado's
"Joint Line," August 23, 1988. Photo: Steve Patterson.

STEEL RAILS ACROSS AMERICA

Gary W. Dolzall and Mike Danneman

Text: Gary W. Dolzall
Design and layout: Mike Danneman
Editor: Bob Hayden
Assistant Editor: Marcia Stern
Production Supervisor: Lawrence O. Luser

DUST JACKET: On Santa Fe's Chicago-West Coast main line, an eastbound intermodal train curls through North Guam, New Mexico, December 29, 1986, in a portrait of modern American railroading. Photo: Joe McMillan.

Distributed to the book trade by:

Tide-mark Press
P. O. Box 8311, East Hartford, CT 06108-0311
ISBN: 1-55949-026-8

PREFACE

THIS BOOK IS CONCEIVED as a celebration — a celebration of the drama and diversity of modern American railroading. In the pages and color photographs that follow, readers will discover that railroading in this country is fascinating, captivating — that there is, as there has been for more than a century and a half, good reason to rejoice in U. S. railroading.

What is it that draws us trackside, that turns us into train-watchers? The answer is different for each of us. Railroading can lure us with the promise of a warm, comfortable Amtrak sleeping compartment and the anticipation of a carefree trip across our continent; railroading can awe us with the fury of potent, howling diesels emerging from a cold, snowy white veil as a Burlington Northern freight challenges the grades and harsh January winds of the Cascade Mountains. Railroading can intrigue us with the spider web of steel rails and the purposeful pattern of signal lights that safely guide scores of daily commuter and passenger trains in and out of Chicago Union Station; railroading can tug at us with its rural beauty, with the gently curving steel rails that carry Conrail trains along the banks of the wide Susquehanna River or steer mile-a-minute Santa Fe freights across the hostile Mojave Desert. Railroading is tradition — exemplified by the grand steam excursion locomotives that still polish American main lines; and railroading is new technology — microprocessor-controlled 4,000-horsepower diesels, Double Stack container trains, and computerized signal systems.

This book cannot definitively document contemporary American railroading; to do so would require far more space. Rather, through color photography, text, and captions, we offer an overview of American railroading, and, most importantly, convey the exciting images and the spirit of today's railroading. To that end, our introductory chapter describes and illustrates the industry. Then, in five regional chapters, we travel the contiguous 48 states (Hawaii has no common-carrier railroads; Alaska's rail system is limited) to witness railroading firsthand, up close. Dividing this country into regions is a subjective exercise — we hope you find our regions at least logical. In a few cases, for the sake of continuity, we've broken our own regional rules — for example, although we've used the Mississippi River as one of the lines of demarcation between the regions presented in Chapters 4 and 5, East St. Louis and St. Louis appear together in the latter chapter.

Join us as we make this journey to discover, to celebrate, to rejoice in the grandeur of American railroading. Join us as we follow the paths of "Steel Rails Across America."

Gary W. Dolzall, Waukesha, Wisconsin
Mike Danneman, Brookfield, Wisconsin
January 1989

Dedicated to all who make railroading great, and to all who cherish it.

CONTENTS

1
AMERICAN RAILROADING:
TRANSITION AND TRADITION

For the train-watcher, the railroad drama lives on

AS THE FINAL DECADE of the twentieth century approaches, railroading is in transition. In an America that is itself in transition — an America trading its legacy of heavy, smokestack industries for a computer-age, service-oriented economy — railroading is, by the hands of necessity and innovation, changing its traditional face.

Change can captivate, or consternate. Many of the age-old, romantic images of railroading are now long into the history books. Steam locomotives (save a precious few preserved and reborn for excursions); elite passenger trains christened *Royal Blue* and *Champion* and *Super Chief*; and fabled companies with corporate titles like Pennsylvania, Seaboard Air Line, Rock Island, and Great Northern are no longer found in this land.

But today, in the footsteps of grand old railroading, walks an industry that mixes timeless traditions with new technology, that commands the attention of train-watchers with rugged-faced, 4,000-horsepower diesel-electrics instead of coal-burning 2-8-2s, that gives names to piggyback hotshots as well as passenger trains — intriguing names like *Expediter* and *Sprint* and *Falcon* and, yes, even *Orange Blossom Special*.

LEFT: Traditional and modern images of railroading mix at historic Horse Shoe Curve as Conrail diesels push tonnage toward the summit of the Alleghenies. Photo: Mike Danneman.

For the modern train-watcher, the sights of traditional railroading — a long, slogging freight train molded of multi-hued boxcars and punctuated by a caboose; a passenger train embarking patrons from the brick platform of a small-town station; a diminutive shortline locomotive carefully waddling down uncertain track — have been joined, often displaced, by new images. And the new images are captivating: potent diesels dragging a chord of long, tri-level auto racks and flat cars loaded with highway trailers over the Alleghenies; a double-deck passenger train, cast in silver, red, white, and blue, twisting up the harsh Front Range of the Rockies; a long, black snake of 100-plus hopper cars carrying 20 million pounds of coal from a Wyoming mine to a Texas power plant; a

titan "Double Stack" train ushering 200 colorful intermodal containers from coast to coast, looking like a 60-mile-per-hour Great Wall of China as it glides across America's heartland.

The Public and the Passenger Train

Railroading today is only vaguely understood by the general public. The man on the street seldom equates railroading with hauling the necessities of his daily life, and can't begin to appreciate the industry's awesome accomplishment of moving 1.3 billion tons of autos and lumber and grain and coal and you-name-it across this vast country every year.

Instead, to the public railroading most often means

late 1960s, when passenger train discontinuances and declining levels of service were the norm, riding the rails on occasion has once more become an accepted, even an "in" thing to do.

And why not? Those commuter agencies have provided long-overdue funding for new or rebuilt equipment and improved suburban trains from Boston to Chicago to San Francisco. After a decade and a half of life, Amtrak stands on stable turf, freed of the annual budget reductions it suffered in the 1970s, and offering rail service on roughly 23,500 of America's 181,000-mile railroad system. Amtrak now owns its busiest route (the multi-track Boston-New York-Washington Northeast Corridor), has molded its New York state and Los Angeles-San Diego corridors into success stories, and has re-equipped its long-distance trains with new or rejuvenated equipment. Aboard carriages variously stenciled "Amfleet" and "Metroliner" and "Turboliner" and "Heritage Fleet" and "Superliner" Amtrak today carries more than 20 million passengers a year. Americans may not entirely comprehend their railroads, and may not board their trains in numbers comparable to travelers in Britain or France or Japan, but arguably this country still cherishes their presence.

The Super Seven

Tonnage. It is the lifeblood of American railroading. As Amtrak's presence on less than 15 percent of this country's present rail system suggests, it is in hauling freight — in annually toting 5.4 million carloads of coal and 1.4 million loads of chemicals and 1 million loads of autos and 5.1 million truck trailers and containers, and more — that the future of America's railroads rests. And by its sheer volume, by the immensity of the task, and by an enduring diversity, freight railroading offers extraordinary drama to the train-watcher who seeks it out.

As we near the 1990s, America's freight railroad scene comprises seven Goliaths, a handful of middleweights, and literally hundreds of supporting players. Christened the "Super Seven," America's biggest freight carriers are the merged, absorbed, and rationalized survivors of a modern consolidation movement that, over the past several decades, has erased company names rich in history — names like Baltimore & Ohio and Atlantic Coast Line and New York Central and Burlington Route.

Taken together, the Super Seven account for roughly 85 percent of America's 147,000 Class 1 rail route-miles (a Class 1 railroad, as defined by the Interstate Commerce Commission, is a company with at

carrying people, and the reaction of those people (shared by many train-watchers) is one of ambivalence. To many, the words "passenger train" recall only the demise of the *20th Century Limited* or *Morning Hiawatha* or *Chief.* The words also recall the red-ink plunge of railroading's once-proud streamliners into the public sector — into America's government-subsidized national passenger railroad, Amtrak, in 1971. Or perhaps the words conjure up the myriad of tax-supported regional commuter agencies bearing curious initials like MARC and MBTA and Metra.

Despite all that, America's public, and most certainly its train-watchers, have chosen not to forsake the passenger train, not to abandon the railroad experience. Compared, at least, to the dark days of the

ABOVE: Short train; big railroad. On Burlington Northern — America's second-longest railroad — short, swift *Expediter* trains offer truck-competitive, regionalized intermodal services. Near Milledgeville, Illinois, September 5, 1987, a Twin Cities-to-Chicago *Expediter* scurries east behind tiger-striped EMD GP50 3151. Photo: Gary W. Dolzall.

least $88.5 million in annual operating revenue), claim some 90 percent of the industry's $26 billion annual revenue, and employ about 80 percent of railroading's quarter-million employees.

Who are these corporate titans, in size and map and purpose? The roll call, in alphabetical order:

Burlington Northern: Born of the 1970 merger of the Burlington, Great Northern, Northern Pacific, and Spokane, Portland & Seattle, further expanded by acquisition of the Frisco (St. Louis-San Francisco) in 1980, BN is America's second-largest railroad at 23,476 miles (in 1988). Stretching from Chicago west to Colorado and Wyoming, northwest to Minneapolis and St. Paul and on to the Pacific Northwest, and south to Texas and even into Alabama and western Florida, BN is perhaps America's most diverse railroad. Coal from Wyoming's Powder River Basin, transcontinental and regional intermodal container and piggyback traffic, grain, and lumber all move behind Burlington Northern's Cascade Green diesels.

Conrail: Created in 1976 amid the shambles of the failed Penn Central merger (of Pennsylvania, New York Central, and New Haven in 1968), Conrail also took in the remains of other failing eastern roads, including Erie-Lackawanna, Lehigh Valley, Reading, and Central of New Jersey. Given an infusion of $2.1

billion by the U. S. Congress and freed of unprofitable commuter operations by regional agencies, in the 1980s Conrail rose phoenix-like to profitability — and private ownership. Stretching 13,300 route-miles from the shores of the Atlantic through the industrial East and Midwest to Chicago and St. Louis, Conrail has developed into a major transcontinental and regional intermodal carrier that also relies heavily upon steel, autos, coal, and grain traffic.

CSX Transportation: Spun from a complicated spider web of corporate consolidations, CSX includes the routes of several fabled roads, including Baltimore & Ohio, Chesapeake & Ohio, Seaboard Coast Line, Louisville & Nashville, and Clinchfield. Although it stretches more than 21,000 route-miles of railroad over most of the East, South, and Midwest, CSX — as did many of its predecessors — still relies heavily upon bituminous coal from Appalachian mines for its lifeblood, and mixes in steel, automobiles and auto parts, grain, chemicals, and intermodal traffic to generate its mammoth ($4.6 billion in 1987) operating revenues.

Norfolk Southern: Often cited as one of America's best managed corporations of any kind, 17,000-mile NS was formed in 1982 by consolidating heavyweights Norfolk & Western and Southern Railway.

Text continued on page 17

ABOVE: Like many of its predecessors — including Baltimore & Ohio, Chesapeake & Ohio, Louisville & Nashville, and Clinchfield — CSX Transportation rejoices in carrying coal. South of Gainesville, Georgia, in July 1987, CSX diesels draw hoppers over the old Gainesville Midland. Photo: Steve Glischinski. BELOW: Symbolic of today's profitable Conrail is the blue fury of an eastbound TV (trailer van) train behind GE B36-7 5050 hustling over Conrail's ex-New York Central main near Otis, Indiana, October 9, 1988. Photo: Gary W. Dolzall.

PRECEDING PAGES: In urban settings from Boston to San Francisco, commuter trains carry tens of thousands of Americans to and from work. The elderly but elegant EMD E units and bi-level, stainless-steel coaches that populate Burlington Northern's famed three-track "raceway" between Chicago and Aurora, Illinois, are among this nation's most stylish suburban trains. Outbound from Chicago at Highlands, July 2, 1988, BN E9 9904 glides west. Photo: Gary W. Dolzall.

RIGHT: Born of the 1982 consolidation of giants Norfolk & Western and Southern Railway, Norfolk Southern is railroading's chief proponent of RoadRailers — specially equipped truck trailers that ride the rails without flat cars. On rainy September 24, 1988, an NS Atlanta-Detroit "Triple Crown" RoadRailer gallops through Walton, Kentucky, behind a GP50 wearing NS's "Thoroughbred" livery. Photo: Gary W. Dolzall.

Few if any faces in railroading are more famous than that of Santa Fe: Witness this trio of yellow "warbonnet" GP60s tugging a Double Stack train up the 1.1 percent grade of Edelstein Hill, west of Chillicothe, Illinois, June 4, 1988. Double Stack trains — carrying intermodal containers two-high on special articulated cars — are one of the marvels of railroading. Photo: Mark Danneman.

Text continued from page 12

Casting its rails from Washington, D. C., through the Southeast to New Orleans, and from Buffalo through the industrial East and Midwest to Chicago and Kansas City, NS has effectively mixed the Appalachian coal dynasty of traditional N&W with Southern's fast-stepping, service-oriented style, becoming a major player in moving both heavy tonnage and intermodal traffic.

Santa Fe (formally, Atchison, Topeka & Santa Fe): Thwarted by the ICC in an attempt to merge with another titan, Southern Pacific, in the mid-1980s, Santa Fe is the lone member of the Super Seven not involved in a major merger in the last two decades. AT&SF's only acquisition, in fact, was the 1984 purchase of 300-mile Toledo, Peoria & Western, which it subsequently resold in 1989. At 11,400 miles Santa Fe is the smallest of the big seven, stretching its primary routes from Chicago southwest to Colorado, Texas, Los Angeles, and San Francisco. Perhaps more than any other railroad in this country, Santa Fe has transformed itself into a fast conveyor belt for intermodal traffic and other time-sensitive tonnage.

Southern Pacific Lines: Grandchild of Leland Stanford's Central Pacific, the road that met Union Pacific at Promontory, Utah, on May 10, 1869, for the driving of the Golden Spike, Southern Pacific is a historic, but recently troubled, railroad. After its failed merg-

On Southern Pacific's tradition-rich New Orleans-Houston-Los Angeles Sunset Route, a quartet of state-of-the-art GE B39-8s hums through Simonton, Texas, with multihued Double Stacks in tow, November 4, 1988. Photo: Reid McNaught.

ABOVE: In the dawn light of May 28, 1988, at Promontory Point, Utah, on Southern Pacific's Overland Route, a westbound freight rolls across the Lucin Cutoff, navigating Great Salt Lake in a display of the timeless glory of railroading. Photo: Blair Kooistra. **BELOW:** On America's biggest railroad — 24,074-mile Union Pacific — a freight departs Salt Lake City behind EMD SD60 6004 in January 1987. The great Western transcon was chartered by the United States Congress 125 years earlier. Photo: Dave Gayer.

er with Santa Fe, Southern Pacific was purchased in 1988 by the much smaller Rio Grande (which effectively began folding itself into SP). By combining SP, its long-time subsidiary Cotton Belt (St. Louis Southwestern), and Rio Grande, the "new" Southern Pacific Lines stretches 15,000 route-miles of railroad from St. Louis, Kansas City, and New Orleans via three routes to the Pacific coast.

Union Pacific: Chartered by act of Congress in 1862, Union Pacific is the most time-honored of the big names in American railroading. But the traditional UP, which pushed ribbons of steel from Council Bluffs and Kansas City west to Los Angeles and to the Pacific Northwest, has grown dramatically in the past decade. In 1981 UP merged with Western Pacific and Missouri Pacific, and in 1988 UP brought the Katy (Missouri-Kansas-Texas) into its fold. The resulting 24,074-mile Union Pacific blankets much of the nation's West and is America's biggest railroad in terms of route-miles. Like western competitors BN and Santa Fe, UP is a major intermodal force, plus a carrier of a broad range of commodities, from coal and chemicals to lumber and grain.

Beyond the Super Seven

In the great shadows cast across this land by the Super Seven stand hundreds of smaller freight railroads. But "smaller" is a relative term, and railroading beyond the Super Seven encompasses companies that are truly small and others that are important links in the industry.

Small? Take, for instance, the Louisville, New Albany & Corydon Railroad. Despite the modest promise of its name, the LNA&C operates only between Corydon Junction and Corydon, Indiana — seven miles. The road owns but a single locomotive, a General Electric 45-ton diesel with the name "Betty Sue" stenciled on the side of its cab. But LNA&C carries on (since 1883), toting a few loads each day from its on-line customers to a Super Seven link with Norfolk Southern.

Short lines such as the LNA&C are labeled Class 3 properties by the ICC; the definition is a railroad with annual operating revenue under $17.5 million. Class 3 roads — and there are about 400 of these fascinating companies in this country — are occasionally famous, often obscure. They are down-home country short lines like LNA&C or the 29-mile Lancaster & Chester Railway snuggled away in South Carolina; they are larger, heavier, longer properties such as the 121-mile Chicago & Illinois Midland, a road that every year moves millions of tons of coal and grain and other commodities; they are modest terminal companies, like the Kansas City Terminal, which sends switch engines out to tend a spider web of city track-

At the opposite end of the American railroading spectrum from Super Seven roads like Southern Pacific and Union Pacific are more than 400 smallish Class 3 railroads that offer diversity, and often charm. On Chicago & Illinois Midland, a 121-mile Midwestern coal hauler, EMD diesels sleep away the night at Springfield, Illinois. C&IM 31 is a rare RS1325; only two were ever built and both went to C&IM. Photo: Mike Danneman/Tom Danneman.

age and provides important traffic links for the big names in railroading.

Between the large and small of railroading, between the Super Seven and the Class 3 short lines, fall what might be called the industry's middleweights. Included are a handful of roads that fit Class 1 criteria but aren't big enough to merit super status; large terminal companies (such as Indiana Harbor Belt, Belt Railway of Chicago, or the Terminal Railroad Association of St. Louis); and a growing clan of what are popularly termed "regional railroads."

The remaining Class 1s beyond the Super Seven are, for the most part, rich in tradition, rich in history . . . included are Chicago & North Western, Soo Line, Illinois Central, Kansas City Southern, Grand Trunk Western, and Florida East Coast. They are properties that, by choice or predicament, never became a part of the megamergers that molded the Super Seven. But they have, nonetheless, inevitably been touched by change.

Consider Florida East Coast: Once the stylish speedway by which an armada of passenger trains reached sunny Miami, 500-mile FEC transformed itself into a no-nonsense, cost-effective freight and intermodal carrier to compete with trucks. To do so, FEC rationalized and modernized its property, cast away national labor agreements by establishing two-man train crews (versus a norm of four), and endured a violent strike that began in 1963 and was not formally settled until 1971.

Or take the Soo Line: Traditionally a quiet, go-about-its-business Midwest granger road and tonnage link to Canada, Soo nearly doubled itself — to 7,500 miles — with the 1985 purchase of a trimmed-down, post-bankruptcy Milwaukee Road. Soo then recast itself again by selling off nearly 2,000 miles of property, including much of the "traditional" Soo, to a new regional railroad, Wisconsin Central, Ltd. (more on the subject of regionals later).

In the world of Class 1 middleweights there are relative success stories, among them Chicago & North Western. Once labeled an also-ran granger with little long-term potential, C&NW melded itself through smallish mergers (small, that is, by today's standards), with granger roads Minneapolis & St. Louis (in 1960) and Chicago Great Western (1968), then trimmed away the fat, pushed its way into Wyoming's burgeoning Powder River Basin coalfields, and established its main line between Chicago and Nebraska as the preferred link for Union Pacific's tidal wave of transcontinental intermodal traffic.

But there are also struggles for survival among the middleweights. Probably none is so great as that of this country's youngest Class 1 — Guilford Transportation Industries. Assembled by Pittsburgh financier Timothy Mellon in 1981, Guilford brought together three financially marginal New England roads — Maine Central, Boston & Maine, and Delaware & Hudson. With MEC, B&M, and D&H established as subsidiaries of Guilford, the system stretched an impressive 4,000 route-miles.

By fashioning another subsidiary, Springfield Ter-

Text continued on page 24

The setting — Daytona Beach (Florida) Golf Club — may recall the old, romantic Florida East Coast, but the blue diesels, piggybacks, and auto racks all suggest the progressive, fast-paced, no-nonsense FEC. At 500 miles, FEC is America's smallest Class 1 railroad. Photo: Alex Mayes.

Changing faces. Where once Milwaukee Road orange prevailed, fresh red-and-white Soo Line SD60 6012 draws out of the darkened bore at Tunnel City, Wisconsin, and into the rich twilight of September 20, 1987. Soo Line purchased Milwaukee Road in 1985. Photo: Gary W. Dolzall.

From an also-ran granger road, Chicago & North Western molded itself first into a survivor, then a Class 1 success story. Coal from Wyoming's Powder River Basin and transcontinental intermodal traffic shared with Union Pacific are C&NW's lifeblood. On UP rails in eastern Nebraska, C&NW GP50 5091 points toward home rails, scurrying east with an American President Lines Double Stack train bound for Chicago, July 15, 1987. Photo: Mike Danneman.

ABOVE: The Illinois Central Railroad was chartered in 1851, disappeared with the formation of Illinois Central Gulf in 1972 — then reappeared in 1988. The granger origins of the Illinois Central — and its traditional black paint — are evident as IC SD20 2005 leads grain hoppers south through Buckley, Illinois, January 21, 1989. BELOW: Extending between Detroit, Cincinnati, and Chicago, Class 1 Grand Trunk Western is controlled by one of Canada's railroad giants, Canadian National. At Blue Island, Illinois, December 3, 1988, Grand Trunk EMD GP38AC 6210 aims tonnage east toward the Motor City. Both photos: Gary W. Dolzall.

ABOVE: America's youngest and most troubled Class 1 is Guilford Transportation. Born in 1981, Guilford soon grew to 4,000 miles by marrying Maine Central, Boston & Maine, and Delaware & Hudson, then contracted with the loss of D&H to bankruptcy in 1988. On the B&M east-west main, Guilford trains meet along the Hoosic River at North Pownal, Vermont, February 28, 1988. Photo: Scott Hartley.

RIGHT: White diesels became a trademark of 1,600-mile Class 1 Kansas City Southern beginning in the late 1960s. At Blue Cut, Arkansas, KCS SD40-2 664 and sisters urge tonnage through the Ouachita Mountains, May 30, 1982. Kansas City Southern links its namesake city with eastern Texas and New Orleans. Photo: David M. Johnston.

Regional revival: Glistening yellow and black paint of New York, Susquehanna & Western F45 6370 and the fast-paced charge of westbound Sea-Land Double Stack train SLN-5, running on Conrail trackage rights at Hankins, New York, reveal the can-do spirit of America's moderate-sized, service-intensive regional railroads. Photo: Scott Hartley.

Text continued from page 20

minal (the original ST was a six-mile short line in Vermont), and transferring pieces of its bigger roads to this "fourth" subsidiary, Guilford attempted to sidestep existing union agreements and cut its labor costs. But amid employee strife and court rulings adverse to its strategy, Guilford's map began to unravel in 1988 with the bankruptcy of Delaware & Hudson. With D&H subsequently handed over, at least temporarily, by the ICC to a designated operator — the regional New York, Susquehanna & Western — the crystal ball for Guilford Transportation and railroading in New England became, at best, cloudy.

Regional Railroad Revival

New York, Susquehanna & Western? You say that your memory of that railroad is of an old anthracite coal hauler, of a diminishing, diminutive (only 43 miles by 1976), chronically bankrupt New Jersey road that could barely fend for itself? Today, as the crown jewel in an eastern rail family known as the Delaware Otsego System, NYS&W means big yellow-and-black SD45 and F45 and Dash 8-40B diesels, stack trains — and profits. Welcome to one of the most remarkable stories of railroading in the past decade — the rebirth of "regional railroads."

In 1980 Congress passed the Staggers Act, which deregulated the railroad industry and gave freight railroads new freedom to compete head-to-head against trucks. To compete — with lower freight rates and more responsive service — also meant the Class 1s

needed to sharpen their operations and trim their waistlines. Competitive rate-making put added pressure on the railroads to restructure their age-old labor agreements, and to accelerate the process, ongoing for decades, of cutting away unprofitable miles of track.

America's Class 1 mileage declined from 191,520 route-miles in 1975 (before Conrail was formed) to 169,927 miles in 1979 (on the eve of the Staggers Act) to under 150,000 in 1987. The missing miles? While many have fallen to the eternal silence of abandonment, between 1980 and 1987 no fewer than 160 new shortline and regional railroad companies were formed to carry on where Class 1s stepped away.

Among this nation's Class 1s, no single railroad has been more earnest in trimming itself — and thus more important in the formation of regionals — than the Illinois Central. In the summer of 1972 the IC was 121 years old, 6,760 miles long, and on the verge of a grand expansion and rechristening. In merging that August with the 2,704-mile Gulf, Mobile & Ohio, the railroad took the name Illinois Central Gulf, and through subsequent purchase of several southern short lines the new ICG reached a peak of 9,568 route-miles in 1974. At its zenith ICG cast trackage south from Chicago, along the east side of the Mississippi River to New Orleans and into Alabama; ICG touched St. Louis and Indianapolis and Louisville; ICG pushed westward to Omaha and Kansas City.

Alas, the story of the Illinois Central Gulf was not a happy one. By 1981 the railroad had become an unwanted stepchild to the conglomerate parent it had spawned, IC Industries. Mired in poor financial results year after year, unable to find a super railroad willing to take it as merger partner, ICG began to trim itself. By December 1988 the railroad had, through abandonments and line sales, dieted down to less than a third of its 1974 size — and had been spun away from its corporate parent to independence under its original name, the Illinois Central Railroad.

But in the transformation from IC to ICG and back again, there had, in the Midwest and South, been born no less than five major regional railroads, plus a host of smaller companies. ICG line sales created the 757-mile Gulf & Mississippi and 777-mile Chicago, Central & Pacific in 1985, the 403-mile MidSouth (which has since acquired the Gulf & Mississippi and several short lines) and the 307-mile Paducah & Louisville in 1986, and the 631-mile Chicago, Missouri & Western in 1987. Along with active if less ambitious line sale programs by other Class 1s such as BN, C&NW, NS, and CSX, IC fueled the fires of regional railroading's growth.

Exactly what is a regional railroad? There is no simple answer, really, because the term suggests a philosophy as much as a measure of size. The philosophy: that a moderately sized railroad (let's say from 100 to several thousand miles), with local manage-

ment and with reasonable labor arrangements, can offer more responsive and personalized service to its customers than can a leviathan Class 1. And so names like New York, Susquehanna & Western and Chicago Central and Paducah & Louisville and Wisconsin Central and Montana Rail Link have stepped front row center in the story of American railroading.

In truth, the regional railroad is not new; perhaps, it is more of an idea returned from history. As late as the 1950s, America was rich in what today would be termed regionals — roads such as Lackawanna and Central of Georgia and Monon and Pere Marquette. Most provided grist for mergers in the past three decades, but a few — New England's 494-mile Bangor & Aroostook and 370-mile Central Vermont, Virginia's 114-mile Richmond, Fredericksburg & Potomac, and traditional ore and steel carriers such as 205-mile Bessemer & Lake Erie and 357-mile Duluth, Missabe & Iron Range come to mind — survive today as elders in the growing tribe of regionals.

Coal and Containers

If recent changes to the corporate roll call and map of American railroading have been at a frantic pace, the transition in the industry's everyday scene has been slower, more subtle. On railroading's high iron

Regional tradition: Although it fits the modern regional railroad concept in size and service, Virginia's 114-mile Richmond, Fredericksburg & Potomac is surely no newcomer, with a charter dating to 1834. Blue-and-gray EMD GP35 131 points RF&P train 171 across Powell's Creek, north of Cherry Hill, Virginia, September 12, 1987. Photo: Alex Mayes.

today, tradition mixes freely with the images of change.

In recent years railroading has struggled to retain its share of intercity freight traffic. Using the measure of intercity ton-miles (a ton of goods moved a mile equals one ton-mile), the railroads carry about 35 percent of all freight tonnage. Trucks account for roughly 25 percent, pipelines 23 percent, barges and ships about 15 percent, and airlines carry the remainder. The split sounds pretty good until you recall that as recently as the 1960s railroading's share was comfortably over 40 percent.

More than a third of railroad tonnage now comes from one commodity — coal. It comes from the Appalachians, from the hills of the Southeast and Midwest, from the yawning strip mines gouged in the grassy plains of Wyoming. In huge hoppers and gons, coal — as much as 100 tons of it per car — is hauled to feed the power plants and industrial furnaces of America. Today, coal most often moves in looming, serpentine (dare we say awesome) unit trains, 100 cars strong, with 12,000 or more diesel horsepower applied to the front drawbar. Hauling coal is a vital part of American railroading's present and its future — yet coal is as closely linked to railroading's past as the steam locomotives that once not only hauled coal but also burned it.

In contrast to its age-old links with coal is railroading's new intermodal alliance with piggyback trailers and shipping containers. Sure, Nickel Plate and Chicago Great Western and a handful of other roads occasionally loaded truck trailers onto wooden flat cars back in the steam era, but "intermodal," perhaps more than any other single word, implies a bright future for railroading. It suggests expansion and innovation; it suggests a willingness to compete. Intermodal trailers and containers can carry virtually any commodity, from televisions to vegetables to books, and can serve any customer, on or off the railroad.

In 1961 the railroads carried fewer than a million trailers and containers; a decade later, 2.2 million; in

King coal, east and west: More than one-third of railroad tonnage today is coal. LEFT: At Mance, Pennsylvania, October 22, 1988, on CSX's ex-Baltimore & Ohio Sand Patch Grade, a trio of CSX EMD diesels strains to lift loaded hoppers westward toward the summit of the Alleghenies. Photo: Gary W. Dolzall. ABOVE: On Colorado's "Joint Line" — owned by Rio Grande and Santa Fe and also used by Burlington Northern — a unit coal train slogs south near Palmer Lake, July 14, 1987. Blue-and-white SD60 diesels are owned by Oakway, Inc., carry markings of builder Electro-Motive, and are leased to Burlington Northern. Photo: Mike Danneman.

The gargantuan stature of Double Stack trains is evident as twin Union Pacific GE Dash 8-40C diesels lend their collective 8,000 horsepower to the march of a westbound K-Line train curling along the Overland Route through desolate Wyoming, October 1988. Photo: Blair Kooistra.

1981, 3.1 million; and in 1987, more than 5 million. Today, intermodal business continues its growth, and ranks second only to king coal in railroading's list of traffic.

Joining the railroads' original methods of moving trailers and containers — TOFC (trailer-on-flat car) and COFC (container-on-flat car) — have, in the past decade, come Double Stacks (containers carried two high on special articulated cars), Fuel Foilers (lightweight, skeleton flats), and RoadRailers (special truck trailers that can be coupled together and ride the rails, without a flatcar).

Intermodal trains are the elite of modern railroading, and to railroader and train-watcher alike, their names and symbols are magic. *Expediter* on BN, *Sprint* on Soo Line, *Falcon* on C&NW/UP, *Q-Train* on Santa Fe, and *TV* (for trailer van) on Conrail — all reflect intermodal race horses, mile-a-minute speeds, and an urgency in moving trains over the railroad that once was reserved mostly for flagship passenger trains.

Arguably, there is no sight in modern railroading more impressive than Double Stack trains — hulking, leviathan creatures that serve as unequaled land transporters of goods. For an ever-growing number of steamship companies — among them American President Lines and Sea-Land (owned by CSX Transportation) — the stack trains serve as a land bridge across the North American continent, linking Atlantic and Pacific ports, tying American cities to industries worldwide.

The Trackside Experience

Train-watchers have always been preoccupied with locomotives. It was true in the steam era, it is true today. The steam locomotive, in the context of everyday railroading, is, of course, now only a memory. The diesel served notice of its intentions to displace steam half a century ago, and a quarter century has passed since America's Class 1 railroads last called steam locomotives to regular toil in places named Paducah and Roanoke.

That excursion steam locomotives — magnificent machines known to train-watchers by initials and numbers as diverse as N&W 611 and PRR 1361 and

NKP 765 and UP 3985 — still dust the main lines with cinders is cause for celebration. It is a testament to the enduring appeal of railroading's traditions, and to the men and women who have worked to save and restore and share the magic of steam.

For day-to-day railroading and the motive power it employs, change no longer implies the transition from steam to diesel, but rather the switch from elder diesels to diesels born of the computer age. There are about 21,000 locomotives in regular service in the United States. Excepting roughly 100 electrics used in East Coast passenger service and a few specialized coal-hauling operations, all are diesels.

State-of-the-art diesel motive power suggests big,

The diversity of American railroading. BELOW: Snuggled in Norfolk Southern's serpentine yard at Bluefield, West Virginia, coal-burning Norfolk & Western 4-8-4 611 and coal-toting NS diesels mix, June 13, 1985. Photo: Joe McMillan. ABOVE RIGHT: On the main line of the Santa Fe in Chicago, Illinois, Amtrak's Chicago-Los Angeles *Southwest Chief* hurtles past an AT&SF freight led by Electro-Motive GP60 demonstrators, April 19, 1986. Photo: Joe McMillan. BELOW RIGHT: At Elizabeth, New Jersey, where more than 250 passenger trains pass each weekday on the Northeast Corridor, an NJ Transit Jersey Arrow electric boards passengers as Amtrak *Metroliner* train 119 sweeps past behind AEM7 electric 946. Photo: Gary W. Dolzall.

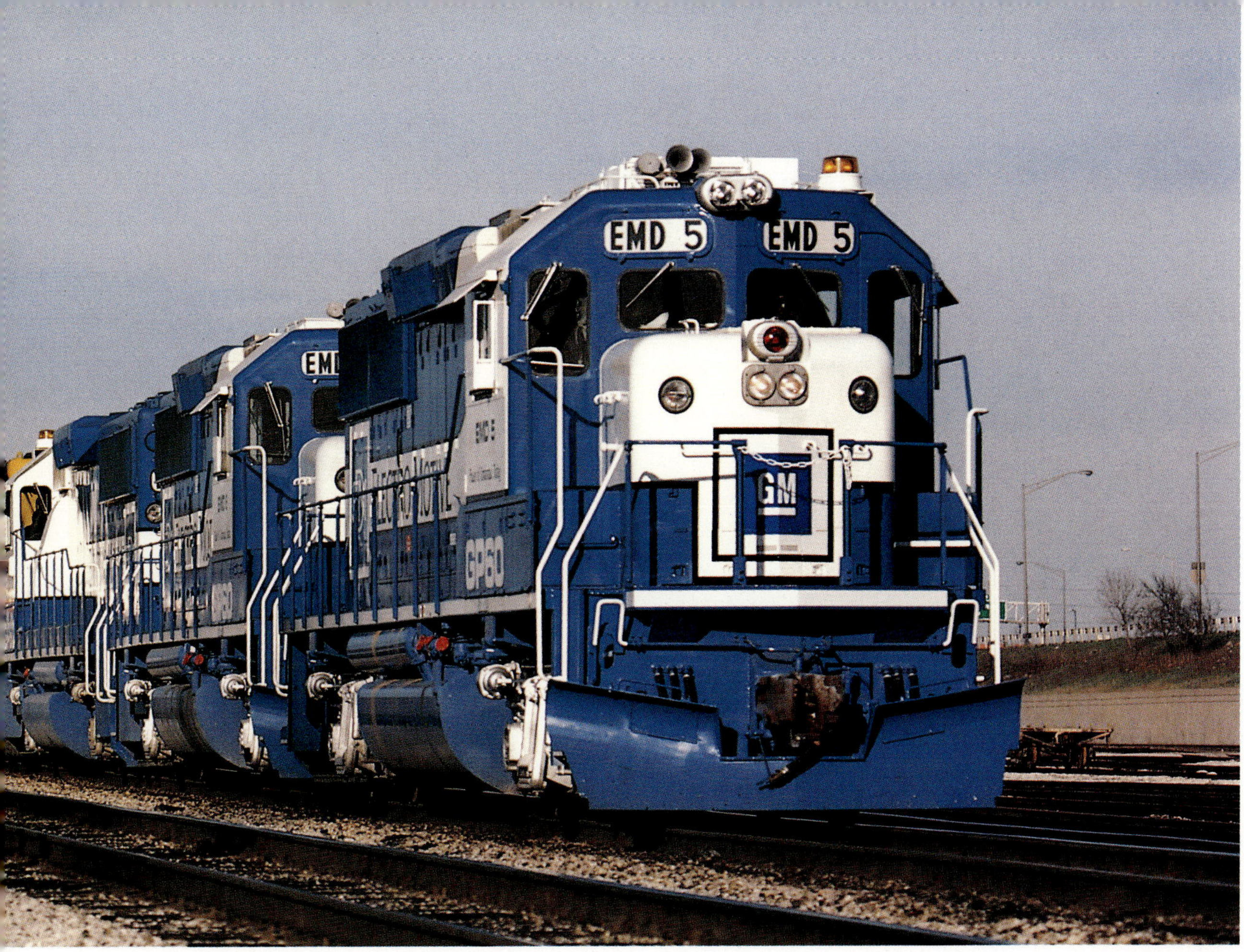
EMD 5
EMD 5
GM
GP60

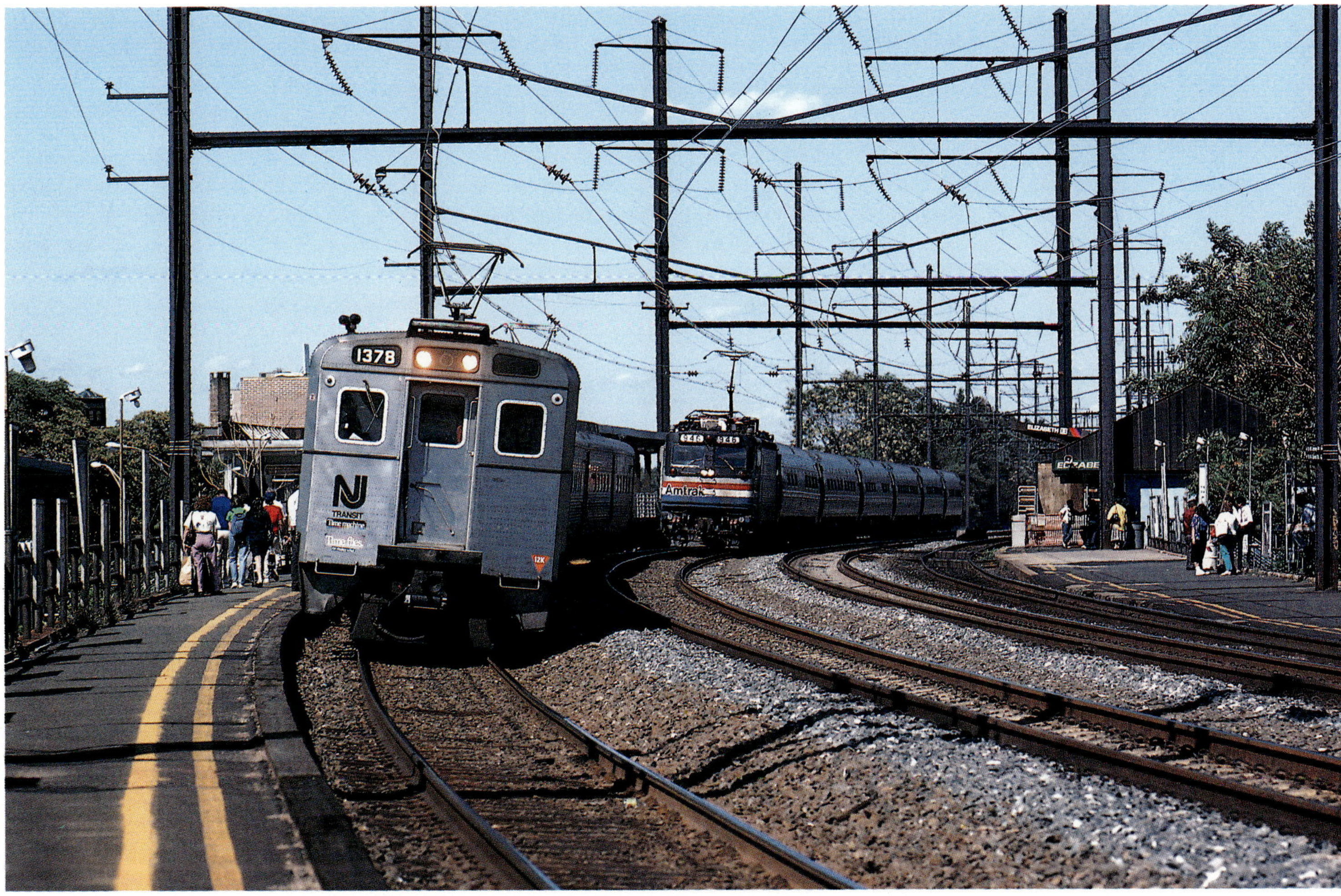
1378
NJ TRANSIT
Amtrak

The unbridled railroad drama awaiting train-watchers is perhaps nowhere more apparent than in the great American West. ABOVE: At Bealville, California, April 24, 1988, seven GE and EMD Santa Fe diesels curl a string of tonnage through the Tehachapi Mountains. Photo: Scott Hartley. RIGHT: Four exhaust-stained Rio Grande EMD diesels headed by GP40 3083 battle the magnificent Front Range of the Rockies at Cliffe, Colorado. Photo: Gary A. Rich.

angular hood units, four or six axles per unit, horsepower as high as 4,000, onboard microprocessors, fuel efficiency, and manufacturer names of General Motors (Electro-Motive Division in the U. S., and GM Diesel Division in Canada) and General Electric. The locomotive language of today reads SD40-2 and GP60, B36-7 and Dash 8-40B.

The diesels that displaced steam, the first-generation streamlined F and E units from Electro-Motive, the orphaned products of Alco and Baldwin and Fairbanks-Morse, have virtually disappeared from the Class 1 freight roads, leaving it to the smaller roads and commuter agencies to preserve the earliest images of dieseldom. The exceptions are those most venerable of diesels — General Motors' first-generation Geeps. Born as the 1,500-horsepower GP7 in 1949, refined as the 1,750-horsepower GP9 five years later, sires of today's hooded diesel titans, these simple, rugged creatures were built by the thousands (6,216, to be exact). Today, only 30 percent of the Class 1 railroads' motive power dates to before 1970, but more than half of the first-generation Geeps still survive (albeit often in rebuilt form) as a vivid link between the dawn of dieselization and today.

Sewing the past to the present — perhaps that is much of the intrigue of railroading. Railroading changes, transforms, yet always offers to willingly recall its heritage. Stand at Horse Shoe Curve, that Mecca for train-watchers in the mountains west of Altoona, Pennsylvania, and you will today witness potent lash-ups of blue-and-white Conrail diesels, straining their combined thousands of horses to lift 10,000-ton freight trains over the Alleghenies. And yet under your feet on that hallowed ground, you will discover a blanket of black cinders, cinders of railroading's past — cinders laid down by the Pennsylvania Railroad 4-8-2s and 2-10-4s that once waged battle with mountains and tonnage, just as the big diesels at Horse Shoe do today.

The railroad experience awaits train-watchers at enduring, historic theaters across this land, at places called Sand Patch and Saluda, Cajon and Tehachapi, Marias and Cascade; it awaits in America's great cities; it awaits at thousands of unremarked hometown grade crossings and hillsides and station platforms from Maine to Iowa to California. The railroad experience remains alive with drama and diversity, calling the train-watcher, as it has for a century and a half, to anywhere that steel rails stretch across America.

2
RAILROADING IN THE NORTHEAST

Where American railroading began, an enduring independence of character

JUST AS DOES OUR COUNTRY, American railroading owes its birth to men who years ago came to the northeast corner of this land, settled it, and molded it. America's first common-carrier railroad, the Baltimore & Ohio, was chartered in its namesake city on February 28, 1827, and B&O's first stone was put in place the following Fourth of July by Charles Carroll, the last surviving signer of the Declaration of Independence.

With the birth of the B&O and the creation of all the properties that followed it — the New York Central and Pennsy, the Erie and New Haven, the Lehigh Valley and Central of New Jersey — railroading became an inseparable, interwoven thread of America's Northeast fabric. And it has remained so ever since.

Now, more than 160 years after the founders of the Baltimore & Ohio first laid down a railroad path, after decades of the industry being shaped, expanded, even overbuilt amid the optimism of nineteenth-century successes, then reforged and reduced by time and inevitable change, railroading in the Northeast still displays an independence of character, a remarkable diversity of style and purpose.

LEFT: Nowhere in America is duplicated the unique drama of the Northeast Corridor. At Elizabeth, New Jersey, an Amtrak *Clocker* hurries toward Philadelphia. Photo: Gary W. Dolzall.

At Northern Maine Junction, near Bangor, June 1, 1980, two generations of EMD diesels —spartan-shaped GP38 88 built in 1967 and stylish F3 42 constructed 20 years earlier — await call on the 494-mile Bangor & Aroostook. Photo: J. David Ingles.

RIGHT: Spinning a path from Montreal to Wells River, Vermont, CP Rail brings Canadian influence to Yankee territory. At Newport Center, Vermont, a CP train is headed by Montreal Locomotive Works RS18 1815. BELOW RIGHT: A less obvious Canadian hand touches the Central Vermont, which through parent Grand Trunk is controlled by giant Canadian National. Central Vermont GP9 4422 leads Alco RS11s across the White River at Sharon, Vermont, in September 1983. Both photos: Scott Hartley.

Consider a few examples: In the far northeastern thumb of this nation, American railroading embraces the long and valued tradition of the 98-year-old, 494-mile Bangor & Aroostook; it abides the influence of Canada's transcontinental giants, Canadian Pacific and Canadian National; and it endures the troubled youth of a Class 1 railroad named Guilford Transportation.

Railroading in the region encompasses colorful, proud short lines — among them the Green Mountain and Lamoille Valley, snuggled away in the scenic isolation of Vermont and New Hampshire — yet it hosts the heavy, dirty, iron-fisted roads that still carve out a living hauling steel and coal and coke, the likes of Pittsburgh's Union Railroad and the Bessemer & Lake Erie and New York's South Buffalo Railway.

Railroading in the Northeast includes the hard, unforgiving, inch-at-a-time struggle of CSX diesels as they lift coal and grain and auto parts and pigs over the rugged path of the old B&O's Allegheny-conquering Sand Patch Grade, and it includes the humming traction motors and sparking pantograph of an Am-

trak AEM7 electric spinning away the miles at 100 per through the New Jersey meadowlands.

If among Northeast railroading's many captivating faces there is a single one that the region can best call its own, it is urban drama. In America's great metropolitan mass stretching from Boston south to New York, Philadelphia, and Washington, D. C., railroading and all its elements become concentrated. For the train-watcher, the images are intense: multiple tracks, overhead wires, crowded, alive stations — and trains, en masse.

In this vast urban concentration that holds nearly a quarter of our country's population, the face of railroading, naturally, tends toward passenger and commuter trains. And with apologies to San Francisco and Los Angeles, and, yes, even to Chicago, there is nowhere in America where the present-day vision of railroads moving people remains so vivid.

Woven from the main lines of the old Pennsylvania and New Haven, Amtrak's Northeast Corridor is alive with bustling Clockers and Metroliners mixed with long-distance trains charging to and from the

RIGHT: Born from the defunct Rutland Railroad in 1963, the Vermont Railway totes trains between Burlington, Vermont, and White Creek, New York. In July 1983, GP38-2 202 tends tank cars at Vermont Railway's headquarters, Burlington.
BELOW: Headed for Ayer on the Boston & Maine's east-west main across Massachusetts, Guilford's Springfield Terminal SD26 623 (once owned by Santa Fe) curls a freight below snow-dressed hills in December 1987. Both photos: Scott Hartley.

ABOVE: On Amtrak's Springfield (Massachusetts)-New Haven (Connecticut) route, once part of the old New Haven, an EMD F40PH hustles train 495 across the Farmington River at Windsor, Connecticut, en route to a Northeast Corridor connection. Photo: Scott Hartley.

Midwest and South, with AEM7 and E60 electric motors, with the enduring bustle of edifices named South Station (Boston) and Penn Station (New York) and 30th Street (Philadelphia) and Washington Union Station.

The Northeast's commuter carriers are legion: Boston's Massachusetts Bay Transportation Authority (MBTA); the trio of Metro-North, NJ Transit, and long-lived Long Island serving the New York metro area; Philadelphia's Southeastern Pennsylvania Transportation Authority (SEPTA); and Baltimore/ Washington's Maryland Area Rail Commuter Services (MARC). Together, over an urban spider web of steel rails, each weekday they issue an armada of diesel- and electric-hauled trains, multiple-unit electrics, and Budd diesel rail cars. Trains as uncommon as MBTA's F-unit-hauled RDCs, Metro-North's squat blue-and-silver electric m.u.s, Long Island's push-pull commuters with Geeps on one end and old Alco cab units on the other, NJT's Jersey Arrows, and spiffy SEPTA and MARC AEM7-powered suburban trains call at stations as diverse as Haverhill and Yonkers, Montauk and Long Branch, Fox Chase and Brunswick, carrying people to and from work.

The nearly endless community cast along the

Gleaming Conrail GE diesels approach the ragged rock portal of State Line Tunnel at Canaan, New York, September 24, 1988, on what once was New York Central's fabled Boston & Albany subsidiary. Ahead for this eastbound Selkirk (New York) to Worchester (Massachusetts) freight is a climb over the scenic and rugged Berkshire Hills. Photo: Scott Hartley.

Northeast's Atlantic shore caters to, indeed demands, the passenger train, yet the region remains a siren for tonnage, too. There is no denying that the industrial glory of the Northeast is much diminished. As heavy industries and coal mines and steel mills between the coast and the inland cities of Pittsburgh and Buffalo have shut down, miles of rail lines have gone rusty. Along a myriad of routes once inked on the corporate maps of companies initialed CNJ and LV and DL&W and L&HR, only memories of past glory now linger. But there remain, too, steel rails constantly polished to silver, rails buffed by the passing flanged wheels of flats and hoppers and boxcars, by the endless movement of tonnage.

Consider the freight traffic on the Northeast's dominant railroad, Conrail. Stand trackside for a day at Buffalo, on Conrail's ex-New York Central main line, and you'll likely witness 50 or more freights — 50 or more urgent passings of big GM and GE diesels hustling intermodal trains and manifest freights between the eastern seaboard and America's heartland. Then venture south, to Conrail's ex-Pennsylvania Railroad east-west main, to the environs of the Allegheny Mountains, to Altoona or Horse Shoe Curve or Gallitzin, Pennsylvania, and you'll discover another 50 or more daily trains — trains carrying coal and steel and ore and grain and lumber, and yes, more containers and trailers.

Today, Northeast freight railroading is favorably symbolized by Conrail (and Susquehanna and CSX and Norfolk Southern) hustling containers and trailers to and from East Coast ports, to and from the intermodal terminals that help feed the great cities' endless appetites for goods.

But freight railroading in the Northeast remains one of many images. It is also a long, serpentine CR

Metro-North: To tens of thousands of commuters, the name implies transport to the bustling concrete canyons of Manhattan, and yet few scenes could appear more rural and peaceful than that of a Metro-North Budd RDC, headed for Bridgeport, Connecticut, kicking up snow as it curls along the Naugatuck River at Beacon Falls, January 24, 1987. Photo: Scott Hartley.

freight slowly lugging itself over the imposing grades of the ancient Berkshire Hills on the fabled Boston & Albany; it is Central Vermont carting lumber south from Canada through the plush Green Mountains and Bangor & Aroostook tending its traditional harvest of Maine potatoes. It is Norfolk Southern dragging steel coils from Pittsburgh and autos across New York state. It is Guilford toting boxcars and tankers and hoppers along the shore of the blue Hoosic River. It is newborn regionals, like the Providence & Worchester and Allegheny Railroad and Buffalo & Pittsburgh, treading ancient steel trails once labeled

NYNH&H and PRR and B&O. It is diminutive Pittsburg & Shawmut and Monongahela extracting coal from the misty Pennsylvania hills. It is short lines such as Massachusetts' Bay Colony and New York's Arcade & Attica and New Hampshire's Claremont & Concord carrying cement and fertilizer and lumber to carve out a fragile living.

In short, Northeast freight railroading — melded and mixed together with its passenger-carting kindred, with Amtrak and NJ Transit and MBTA and SEPTA — promises a grand and enduring show for the modern train-watcher.

ABOVE: With a local freight in tow, Guilford (Springfield Terminal) GP18 41 steps over the Nauga-tuck River at Waterville, Connecticut, on the ex-New Haven Torrington branch. BELOW: Dressed in the snows of February 1988, Guilford (ST) Alco C424 75 endures 1-degree temperatures as it treads through Elnora, New York, on the troubled D&H. Both photos: Scott Hartley.

Regional Providence & Worcester, formed in 1973, operates on more than 300 miles of ex-New Haven and ex-Boston & Maine trackage in Massachusetts, Rhode Island, and Connecticut. In 1985, P&W GP38s worked the Gardner (Massachusetts) B&M interchange. Photo: Scott Hartley.

ABOVE: Massachusetts Bay Transportation Authority (MBTA) F40PH 1013 and Pullman-Standard push-pull coaches glide past aging Signal Tower A as the evening rush begins out of Boston's North Station, July 25, 1986. MBTA handles more than 70,000 commuters daily. Photo: Mike Danneman. RIGHT: 58 miles west of Boston, Conrail GE diesels draw auto racks east along the old Boston & Albany at Charlton, Massachusetts, July 4, 1988. Photo: Scott Hartley.

ABOVE: Few rail landmarks in the Northeast are more famous than Starrucca Viaduct, a 17-arch, 1,040-foot-long sandstone structure near Lanesboro, Pennsylvania, on Conrail's ex-Erie Southern Tier. In October 1987, Conrail diesels stride across the viaduct with Double Stack train TV-305. Photo: John S. Murray. BELOW RIGHT: Another scenic marvel of railroading is Conrail's ex-New York Central River Line, which traces the Hudson River's west bank south from Selkirk, New York. At Fort Montgomery, August 30, 1986, Conrail diesels near impressive Bear Mountain bridge. Photo: Scott Hartley.

PRECEDING PAGES: Spanning the Delaware River at Millrift, Pennsylvania, Susquehanna stack train SLN-5 (a Sea-Land transcon operating on NYS&W from Little Ferry, New Jersey to Binghamton, New York) rolls behind NYS&W GE Dash 8-40Bs and a leased Norfolk Southern C30-7. This line is Conrail's ex-Erie route, which NYS&W utilizes between Campbell Hall, New York, and Binghamton. Photo: Scott Hartley.

Following Delaware & Hudson's 1988 bankruptcy, Susquehanna took over D&H operations (replacing Guilford). On January 14, 1989, yellow-and-black NYS&W GE Dash 8-40Bs pull Delaware & Hudson tonnage through South Schenectady, New York. Photo: Scott Hartley.

ABOVE: Beneath catenary that recalls New York, New Haven & Hartford origins, Metro-North electric m.u. cars race through Riverside, Connecticut, October 20, 1988. Metro-North electrics dash along Amtrak's Northeast Corridor as far north as New Haven, Connecticut. Photo: George W. Hamlin.

LEFT: Under the arch chiseled "Track 23," an Amtrak Turboliner in from Schenectady, New York, rests in Manhattan's famed Grand Central Terminal. GCT is used by Amtrak trains on the ex-New York Central Hudson Line, plus Metro-North commuters. Photo: Gary W. Dolzall. RIGHT: The Hudson Line (along the river's east shore) is owned by Metro-North from New York City to Poughkeepsie, New York. Near Peekskill, EMD FL9s sprint out of Little Tunnel. Photo: Scott Hartley.

51

Gotham! As seen from the cab of an inbound commuter train, EMD FL9 5020 dressed in the livery of Metropolitan Transportation Authority (which operated commuter services prior to Metro-North's 1983 formation) rolls north along the Fifth Avenue Viaduct in Manhattan. Photo: Scott Hartley.

The Long Island became renowned in the 1970s and 1980s as the last regular user of Alco FA cab units. As here at Oyster Bay, New York, the old Alcos serve as power cars and rear control cabs on push-pull trains. Photo: Scott Hartley.

Along with Metro-North and Long Island, NJ Transit provides major services for New York area commuters. ABOVE: At Jersey City, NJ Transit GE U34CH 4167 peeks out of Bergen Tunnel on ex-Lackawanna rails. Photo: Scott Hartley. BELOW: On Amtrak's Northeast Corridor at Elizabeth, August 22, 1988, NJT E60 963 and F40PH 4119 race south, destined for the old New York & Long Branch. Photo: Gary W. Dolzall.

The platform tracks of Washington Union Station are populated on November 11, 1988 with Maryland Area Rail Commuter (MARC) AEM7 4903, a Budd RDC, and a Bombardier-built push-pull coach. Photo: Scott Hartley.

ABOVE: Easing toward the upper level of Philadelphia's 30th Street Station, Amtrak E60 950 tends train 609 bound for Harrisburg, Pennsylvania. Cars are ex-Metroliner m.u. cars, but the E60 has been added for insurance in the wintery weather of January 1987. LEFT: At Wayne Junction, Philadelphia, Southeastern Pennsylvania Transportation Authority (SEPTA) Silverliner III m.u. cars and AEM7 2306 stand together, April 26, 1988. Both photos: Rob Palmer.

Atop CSX's century-and-a-half-old Thomas Viaduct, southwest of Baltimore, the New Jersey-Florida *Orange Blossom Special* piggyback train rolls south behind a mix of Richmond, Fredericksburg & Potomac and CSX diesels, March 7, 1987. Photo: Alex Mayes.

Three of five F9Ms operated by MARC (the units are rebuilt ex-B&O F units lettered for owner Maryland Department of Transportation) congregate at Brunswick, Maryland. MARC operates commuter trains from Washington Union Station west to Brunswick and Martinsburg, West Virginia, and north to Baltimore. Photo: George W. Hamlin.

Gliding over the magnificent steel bridge and trestle that carries Amtrak's Northeast Corridor across the Susquehanna River between Havre de Grace and Perryville, Maryland, Amtrak's Amfleet-equipped *Minute Man* trails behind AEM7 908. Photo: Alex Mayes.

Sand Patch Grade: The crossing of the Alleghenies by CSX's ex-Baltimore & Ohio Cumberland (Maryland)-Pittsburgh (Pennsylvania) main has long drawn train-watchers to scenic and remote southern Pennsylvania. ABOVE: At Mance, on the Alleghenies' east slope, Amtrak's Chicago-Washington *Capitol Limited* eases downgrade, October 22, 1988. Photo: Gary W. Dolzall. RIGHT: Later the same day, a CSX string of auto racks draws around the Mance horseshoe behind three EMD diesels in Chessie dress. Photo: Mike Danneman. ABOVE RIGHT: A CSX westbound freight attains the Allegheny summit and clears the west portal of Sand Patch Tunnel, February 14, 1988. Photo: Alex Mayes.

8619
SEABOARD
SYSTEM
8619
6624

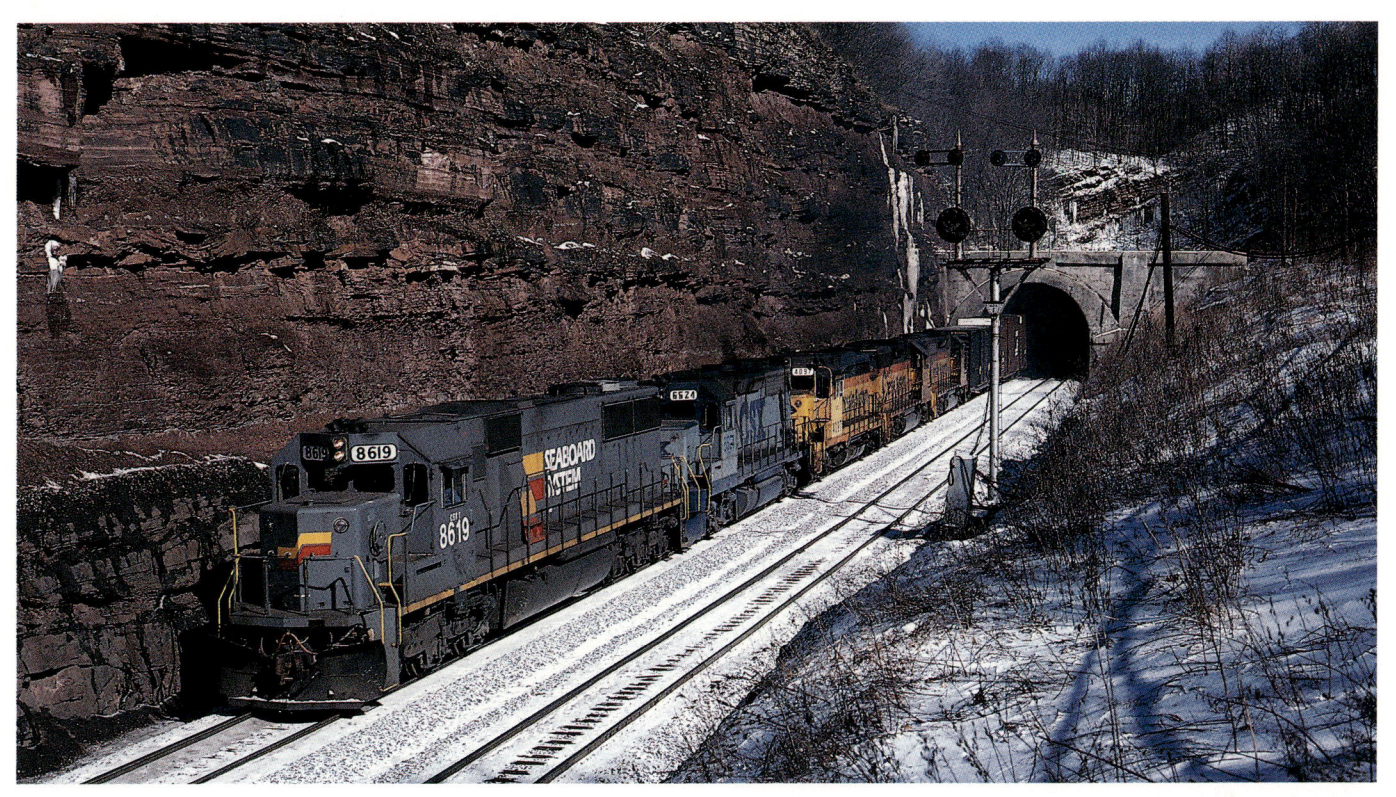

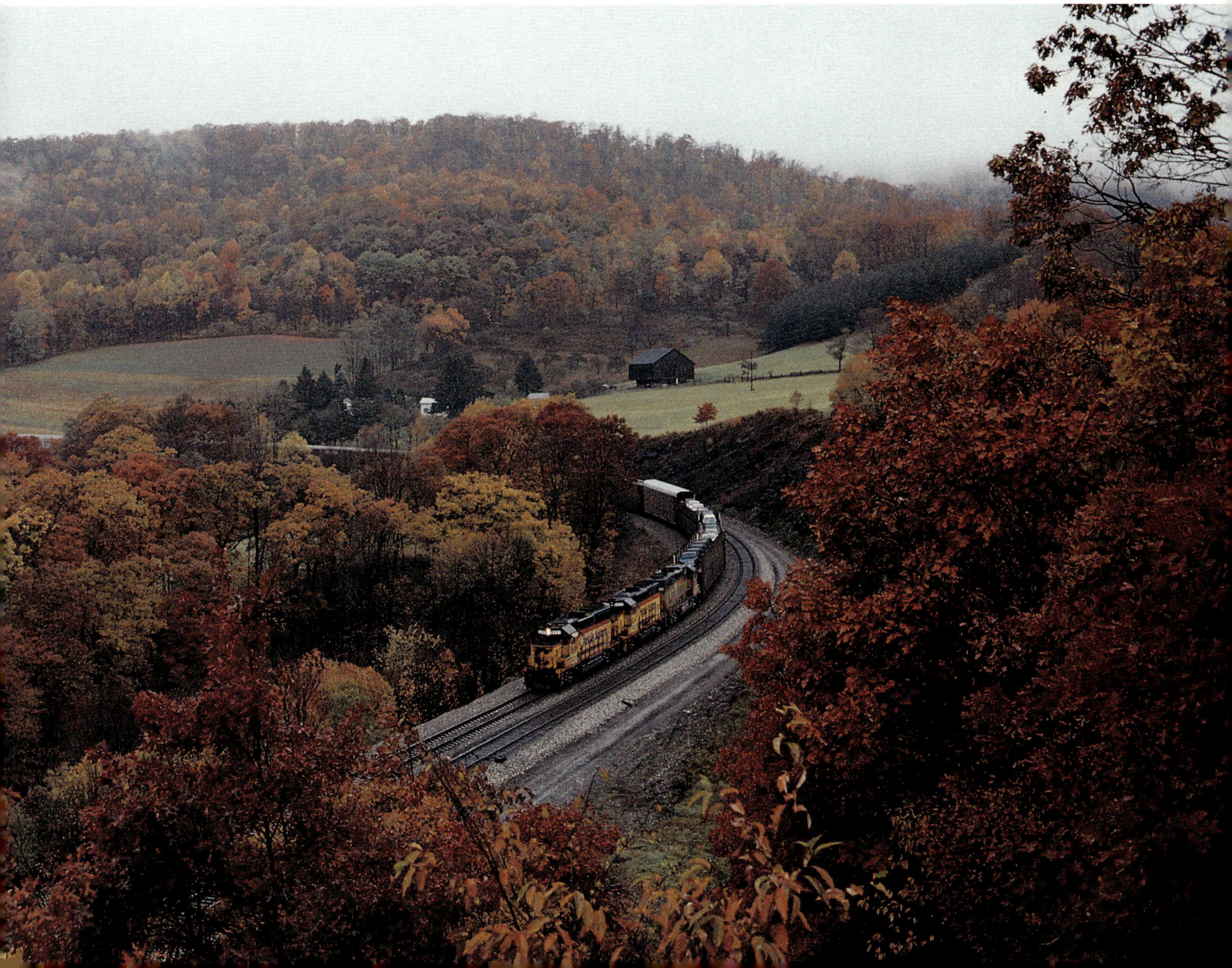

PRECEDING PAGES: Against an Allegheny wall of brilliant autumn color, Conrail GP40-2 3308 brings a loaded coal train down the north rim of Horse Shoe Curve, four miles west of Altoona, Pennsylvania, on CR's ex-Pennsy east-west main line, October 23, 1988. Photo: Gary W. Dolzall.

RIGHT: A Pennsylvania K4 in steam! After nearly three decades of retirement in Horse Shoe Curve's park, PRR 1361, born in 1916, was returned to her Altoona birthplace in 1985 and steamed up in 1987. Splitting fields at Seven Valleys, Pennsylvania, August 27, 1988, the 4-6-2 draws an excursion over Pennsy's old Northern Central Branch, now the Stewartstown Railroad. Photo: Alex Mayes.

LEFT: Arguably the Northeast's — and America's — most famous railroad location, Horse Shoe Curve, hosts a meet between Conrail EMD SD40s dropping downgrade and a westbound intermodal train behind GE B36-7s on October 21, 1988. Photo: Mike Danneman. ABOVE: At Cresson, Pennsylvania, the crew of CR SD50 6710 takes orders at MO Tower as helpers and another freight stand in the distance, December 30, 1985. Photo: John S. Murray.

LEFT: In May 1986, Bessemer & Lake Erie SD18 854 and two SD9s draw coal loads from Republic Mine 2 at Russellton, Pennsylvania. Coal, ore, and steel are staples for B&LE. BELOW: On the old main of the Pittsburgh & West Virginia, Norfolk Southern Geeps glide over the Youghiogheny River at Banning, Pennsylvania, April 19, 1986. In the valley below are the rails of CSX and Pittsburgh & Lake Erie. Both photos: John S. Murray.

LEFT: On Conrail's ex-NYC main through Buffalo, New York, three GEs, headed by Dash 8-40B 5078, scurry a westbound intermodal train past an empty unit coal train. In the distance on this July 1988 day is a Norfolk Southern freight on ex-Nickel Plate track. Photo: John S. Murray.

ABOVE: Easing through Munhall, Pennsylvania, along the Monongahela River, SW1500s of 31-mile Union Railroad lug a hot steel ingot train, May 4, 1986. BELOW: Squeezing down the streets of Elizabeth, Pennsylvania, U28B 2818 of 273-mile Pittsburgh & Lake Erie points hoppers toward Brownsville and a connection with the Monongahela Railroad. Both photos: John S. Murray.

Norfolk Southern SD40-2 6190 cuts through the fog of a May 1985 morn in Pennsylvania's Allegheny Plateau. The EMD and a GE sister are threading their way through Carnegie, Pennsylvania, on track which once belonged to Pittsburgh & West Virginia. Photo: John S. Murray.

3
RAILROADING IN THE SOUTH

In a land dominated by two titans,
visions of coal, fast freights, and reborn steam

IN THAT GREAT ARC OF AMERICA that lies south of the Potomac and Ohio rivers and east of the Mississippi, railroading is today dominated by two of the Super Seven. The route maps of rail titans Norfolk Southern and CSX intermingle and entwine, each blanketing old Dixie from Virginia to eastern Louisiana and from Kentucky to Florida. And why not? In this era of megamergers, shouldn't the two rail giants who choose to call Norfolk, Virginia, and Jacksonville, Florida, their headquarters also call the South their very own?

Is it an overstatement to so closely link the initials NS and CSX with the South? It is true that Norfolk Southern and CSX both venture far from the South. Both pour over the Midwest and even dispatch trains onto Canadian soil. And it is true that the South is not the sole domain of CSX and NS. Super Seven kindred Burlington Northern reaches all the way to Pensacola, Florida, Conrail wanders into West Virginia in search of coal, and the trains of Southern Pacific and Union Pacific call upon Memphis and New Orleans. Middleweight Class 1s Illinois Central, Kansas City Southern, and Florida East Coast; regionals such as Richmond, Fredericksburg & Potomac, MidSouth, and Paducah & Louisville; and a plethora of short lines all place their marks on southern railroading. But without Norfolk Southern and CSX, railroading in the South would simply not be whole, just as surely as neither railroad would be complete without Dixie.

LEFT: In remote eastern Kentucky, priority tonnage hurries along Norfolk Southern's Cincinnati-Chattanooga main line, the bustling "Rat Hole." Photo: Steven Cigolle.

If domination by two railroads sounds uninteresting for the train-watcher, if the South seems shorn of the intrigue and variety of its colorful past, then consider this: While the corporate names and paint schemes and endearing idiosyncracies of the predecessors of NS and CSX — the likes of Southern and Norfolk & Western (which, technically, remain as operating subsidiaries of NS), of Clinchfield, Chessie, and Louisville & Nashville, et al. — may be disappearing, their legacies remain.

In the modern South of NS and CSX, rails still climb Saluda Mountain, rolling up the 5.1 percent grade that's known as the nation's steepest main line, standard gauge railroad; coal trains still snarl through remote communities named Bluefield and Hinton and Corbin on shining rails once tended by N&W and C&O and L&N; nocturnal fast freights still rocket through North Carolina's pine-dotted coastal plains on the steel speedway of the old Atlantic Coast Line; piggybacks still rally through Kentucky and Tennessee, twisting through the rocky cuts of Southern's renowned "Rat Hole." In other words, while the corporate names have changed, the places — and the enduring drama of southern railroading — most often remain.

And then there is the matter of steam. Mainline steam — BIG steam. With all respect to other Class 1s that have sponsored, or at least obliged, the return

Allegheny gateway. At historic Harpers Ferry, West Virginia, Baltimore & Ohio's original main line crosses the Potomac River and strikes out toward the rigors of the Alleghenies. ABOVE: MARC's Washington-Martinsburg (West Virginia) *Blue Ridge* clears Harpers Ferry Tunnel, September 7, 1988, behind GP39H-2 73. Photo: Alex Mayes. RIGHT: Amtrak's Washington-bound *Capitol Limited* crosses the Potomac River at Harpers Ferry, October 14, 1988. Photo: John S. Murray.

of the steam locomotive to their high iron — with apologies to UP and SP and CSX and C&NW — there are no names more synonymous with mainline steam in the modern age than Norfolk Southern and, before it, Southern Railway.

The Dixie miracle that began with Southern 2-8-2 4501 in 1966 has, over the past quarter century, given a high iron stage to steam locomotives as diverse as a Texas & Pacific 2-10-4, a Canadian Pacific Hudson, an ex-C&O 2-8-4. And, since the 1982 marriage of Norfolk & Western and Southern, the NS steam program and the Birmingham (Alabama) shops that give it heart and soul have returned to life two of N&W's iron legends — Class J 4-8-4 611 and Class A 2-6-6-4 1218. If the South's rails recommended nothing more than the steamy breath of svelte 611 and the hooter-whistle of gargantuan 1218, then to many train-watchers all the world would be well.

But, of course, there is much more to modern southern railroading. More than 611 and 1218 and kin.

The traditions of Chessie in West Virginia. LOWER LEFT: The small community of Grafton rests on what was B&O's first mainline crossing of the Alleghenies. In the late 1980s, despite this route's demotion (in favor of the Sand Patch line) to secondary status, Grafton remains alive as a coal-gathering point, witness B&O-clad GP40 3763 tugging hoppers through town in June 1986. Photo: Joe McMillan. LEFT: One of CSX's coal arteries, the Grafton-Richwood branch, hosts CSX EMD diesels slipping across Pleasant Creek Viaduct in October 1987. Photo: George W. Hamlin. BELOW: Farther south, the ex-Chesapeake & Ohio main line burrows through the New River Gorge to stretch its way across the heart of West Virginia. At Quinnimont, Chessie GE B30-7 8238 draws coal under a C&O signal mast. Photo: Joe McMillan.

More, dominance or not, than Norfolk Southern and CSX Transportation.

Take, for instance, two railroads that may be modest in route-miles, but certainly not in style — the Richmond, Fredericksburg & Potomac and the Florida East Coast. There are striking similarities between them — both hug the shore of the Atlantic Ocean, both serve only one state (Virginia for the RF&P; Florida for FEC), both were once passenger speedways that served, respectively, as the north and south bookends in the great Northeast-Florida passenger trade. And today, both are pulsing freight-tonnage race tracks. Yet, there are also dramatic differences in the companies: Both roads have achieved longevity and success, but they have taken far different paths.

The RF&P, 114 miles of mostly double-track main line stretched between Potomac Yard (at Arlington,

Virginia) and Richmond, is, in a manner befitting a company whose charter dates to 1834, bathed in and devoted to tradition. RF&P's blue and gray colors, symbolic of its role as a link between North and South, were once applied to beautiful 4-8-4s. RF&P has always been conservative and refined in a manner consistent with Virginian traditions (in fact, the commonwealth of Virginia is part owner of the road). From 1925 to 1953, RF&P carried a Seaboard Air Line Florida-New York passenger train named the *Orange Blossom Special*; now, another *Orange Blossom Special* — a CSX Florida-New Jersey hotshot pig train — keeps the fabled name alive. And on today's RF&P, amid the passings of the *Orange Blossom Special* piggybacker and other fast-paced tonnage, streamliners — thanks to Amtrak — still polish the rails.

Amtrak trains named *Virginian* and *Potomac*, *Colonial* and *Tidewater*, *Silver Star* and *Silver Meteor*,

In all America, there are few busier tonnage paths than Norfolk Southern's ex-Norfolk & Western main across Virginia and West Virginia. LEFT: East of Bluefield, West Virginia, NS EMD SD40-2 6140 leads a westbound, framed against the splendor of the Appalachians in summer. Photo: Alex Mayes. ABOVE: At Montgomery Tunnel, near Christiansburg, Virginia, westbound empty coal hoppers are drawn back toward the mines behind NS GE diesels. Photo: Ron Flanary. BELOW: Coal, millions of tons of coal carried in countless trains, keeps NS's steel rails polished bright. Near Glen Lyn, Virginia, NS C30-7 8018 passes traditional N&W position-light signals toting eastbound loaded coal hoppers. Photo: Ron Flanary.

Big steam! Stars of Norfolk Southern's steam excursion program are classic Norfolk & Western power — J-class 4-8-4 611 and A-class 2-6-6-4 1218. ABOVE: In West Virginia, N&W 611 erupts from Cooper Tunnel and rolls onto NS's mainline bridge over the Bluestone-Widemouth branch. Photo: Joe McMillan. ABOVE RIGHT: In April 1987, massive, articulated N&W 1218 fills the skies of Virginia's Blue Ridge with fragrant bituminous coal smoke. Photo: Reid McNaught.

Palmetto and *Auto-Train* all scurry over RF&P. In fact, *Auto-Train*, which carts not only passengers but also their automobiles between the Northeast and Florida, makes Lorton, Virginia, on the RF&P, its northern terminus.

Nearly 700 rail miles south of Richmond lies Jacksonville, Florida, north end of the Florida East Coast. Unlike RF&P, the FEC today carries not a single passenger — all of Amtrak's Florida trains stay on CSX rails. And the FEC has no time or inclination to recall its traditions. Its deep blue diesel hood units suggest strictly business; never mind the ornate red and yellow passenger livery of the FEC diesels that once forwarded the *Florida Special* and *Dixie Flagler*. What was once double-track is now largely single-iron on concrete ties, CTC-signaled. For its 500 route-miles between Jacksonville and Miami, FEC is, simply, a machine. A well-oiled, lean, effective machine. FEC's game is to challenge the truckers on parallel Interstate 95 and beat them often enough to prosper. For the last two decades FEC has done just that.

Due to the South's growing population and industrial bases, due to the great bituminous coal reserves stretching from West Virginia to western Kentucky, southern-style railroading is as solvent, as prosperous, as can be found in any region of the United States. Thanks in no small part to pulpwood, paper, and chemical traffic, the Deep South is also rich beyond its measure in short lines. Captivating short lines with names like Aberdeen & Rockfish and Ashley, Drew & Northern and Columbus & Greenville and Meridian & Bigbee enrich the pages of *The Official Railway Guide*. The fact that troubled Class 1 Illinois Central Gulf trimmed itself heavily in the South only added to this diversity, bringing forth regionals such as MidSouth and Paducah & Louisville.

For the train-watcher, the South awaits with the drama of coal trains daring the most remote Appalachian gorges, with the warm winds and palm trees of Florida, with the down-home nature of rural short lines, with the mile-a-minute charges of intermodal speedsters, from pig trains to Double Stacks to RoadRailers. For the train-watcher, the American South is, simply, a grand stage for modern railroading.

Action on the RF&P. ABOVE: Silhouetted against an angry January 1987 sky, RF&P and CSX diesels cross Neabsco Creek, south of Woodbridge, Virginia, with an intermodal train. Photo: George W. Hamlin. FAR RIGHT: Leaning into a curve at Franconia, Virginia, RF&P GP40 143 heads the Florida-bound *Orange Blossom Special* in March 1987. Photo: Alex Mayes. RIGHT: Its journey from Florida nearly complete, Amtrak's *Auto-Train* rolls along the Potomac River, near Possum Point, Virginia. Power is a pair of GE-built P30CH diesels. Photo: Alex Mayes.

ABOVE: One of the numerous scenic landmarks on the old Clinchfield, Copper Creek Viaduct, near Speers Ferry, Virginia, feels the weight of three CSX diesels (all wearing Family Lines livery) in March 1988. RIGHT: The tunnel is the work of Mother Nature, the tracks those of Norfolk Southern, the train belongs to CSX. At Natural Tunnel, Virginia, where Stock Creek carved this 850-foot bore perhaps a million years ago, a CSX coal train utilizes NS trackage rights as it works south from Big Stone Gap, Virginia, to Frisco, Tennessee, in October 1987. Both photos: Ron Flanary.

PRECEDING PAGES: From the darkened, jagged rock interior of Tunnel 29 on the ex-Clinchfield Railroad at Speers Ferry, Virginia, a southbound CSX coal train behind worn EMD SD40-2 8114 returns to summer daylight, June 14, 1987. Photo: Ron Flanary.

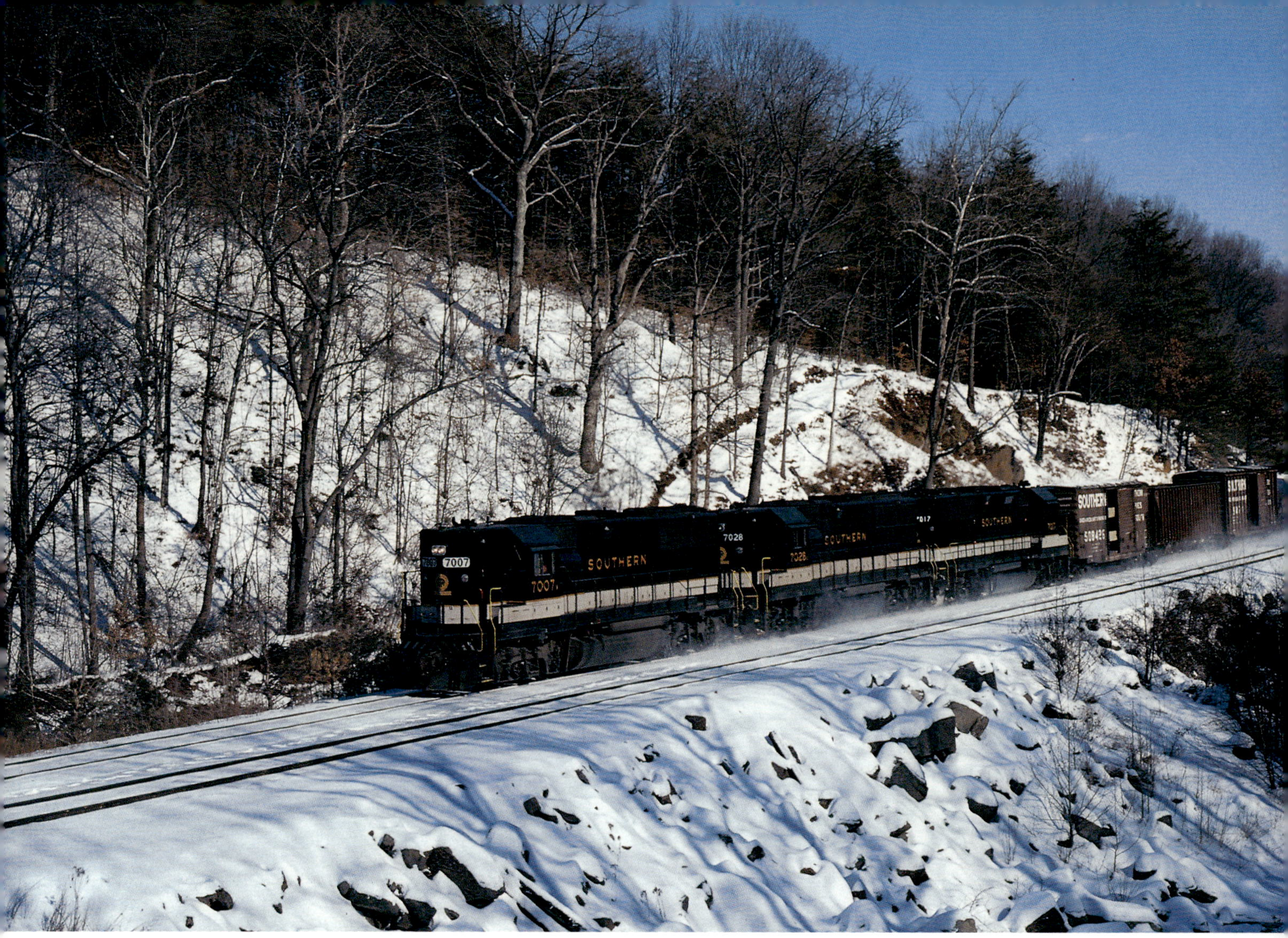
7007
SOUTHERN
7028
SOUTHERN
SOUTHERN
SOUTHERN

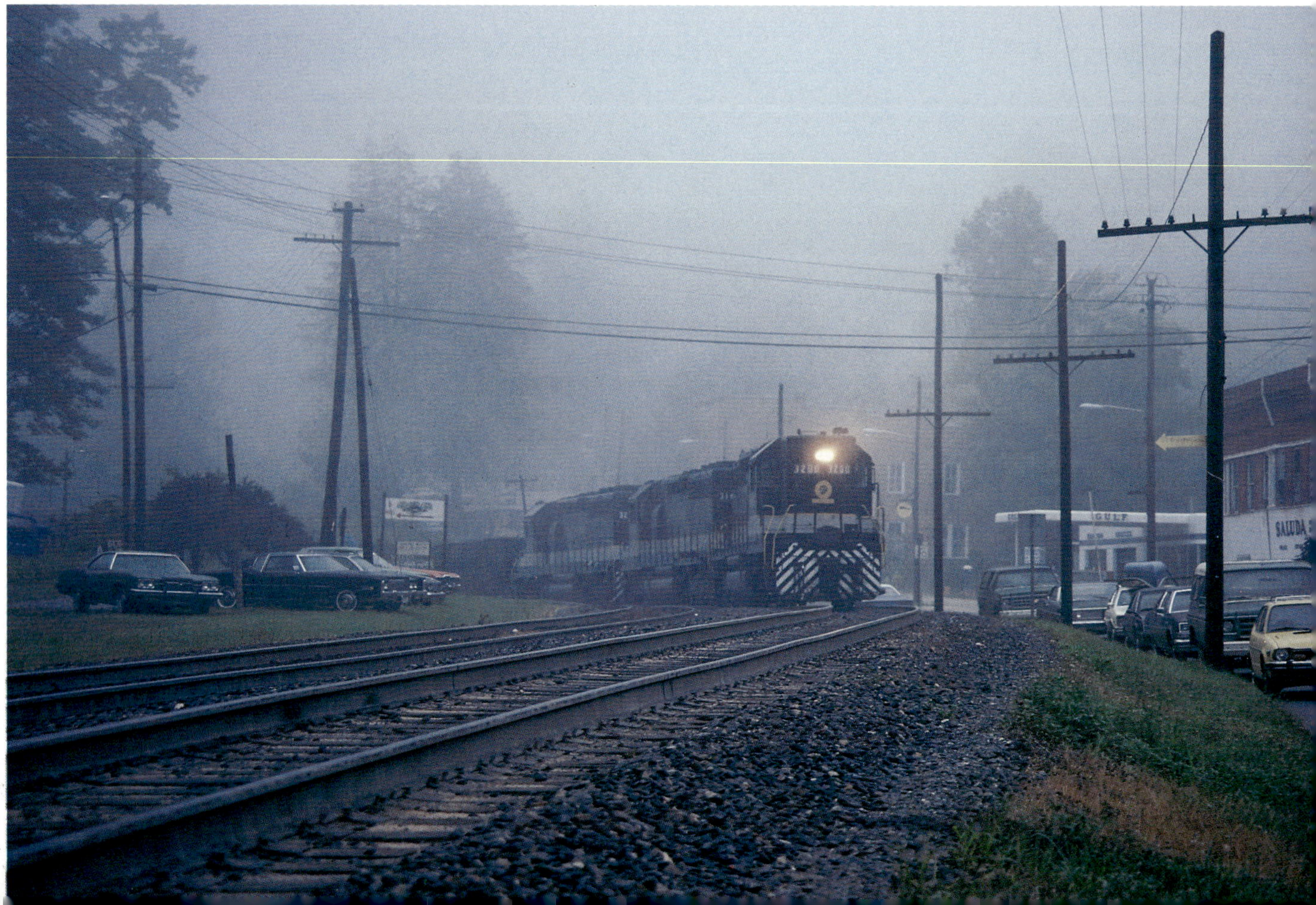
GULF

ABOVE: A marked contrast to 17,000-mile Norfolk Southern is 18-mile Winchester & Western, which operates between Gore and Winchester, Virginia. Hauling the short line's prime commodity — sand — W&W Alco S6 diesel switchers nonetheless provide ample verve as they struggle up-grade with covered hoppers on May 10, 1985. Photo: Alex Mayes.

ABOVE LEFT: On Norfolk Southern's Washington-to-Atlanta main line, snows are not common, but on January 6, 1982, Southern-clad EMD GP50s swirl up a wintery veil of white as they forward tonnage near Clifton, Virginia, 28 miles south of America's capital city. Photo: Alex Mayes.

LEFT: On a foggy morn, Norfolk Southern SD40s tip over the summit at Saluda, North Carolina, with a southbound coal train. Ahead is a careful, 8-mile-per-hour crawl down the 5 percent grade of America's steepest main line. Photo: Gary W. Dolzall. ABOVE: In the same state, yet in a far different setting, Norfolk Southern GP38-2 5075 wanders with 12 cars in tow through the flatlands along NS's 27-mile High Point-Asheboro branch. Photo: Mike Small.

Steel rails and blue Florida waters. RIGHT: At Sanford, CSX intermodal train 181 steps across the St. Johns River, on what once was Atlantic Coast Line's Jacksonville-Tampa main. Lead unit, still in Seaboard System paint, is a GE B36-7. Photo: Alex Mayes. BELOW: Hauling locally mined phosphate (for use in fertilizer) has been a staple of railroading in western Florida since the steam era. Chugging across the Alafia River in East Tampa, GE U36B 5805 and an engineless "Mate" pull phosphate loads toward Tampa Bay. Photo: Scott Hartley. BELOW RIGHT: On the east coast of Florida, atop a graffiti-covered trestle, Florida East Coast GP40-2s spin through Melbourne with the third section of FEC train 96, October 16, 1988. Photo: Alex Mayes.

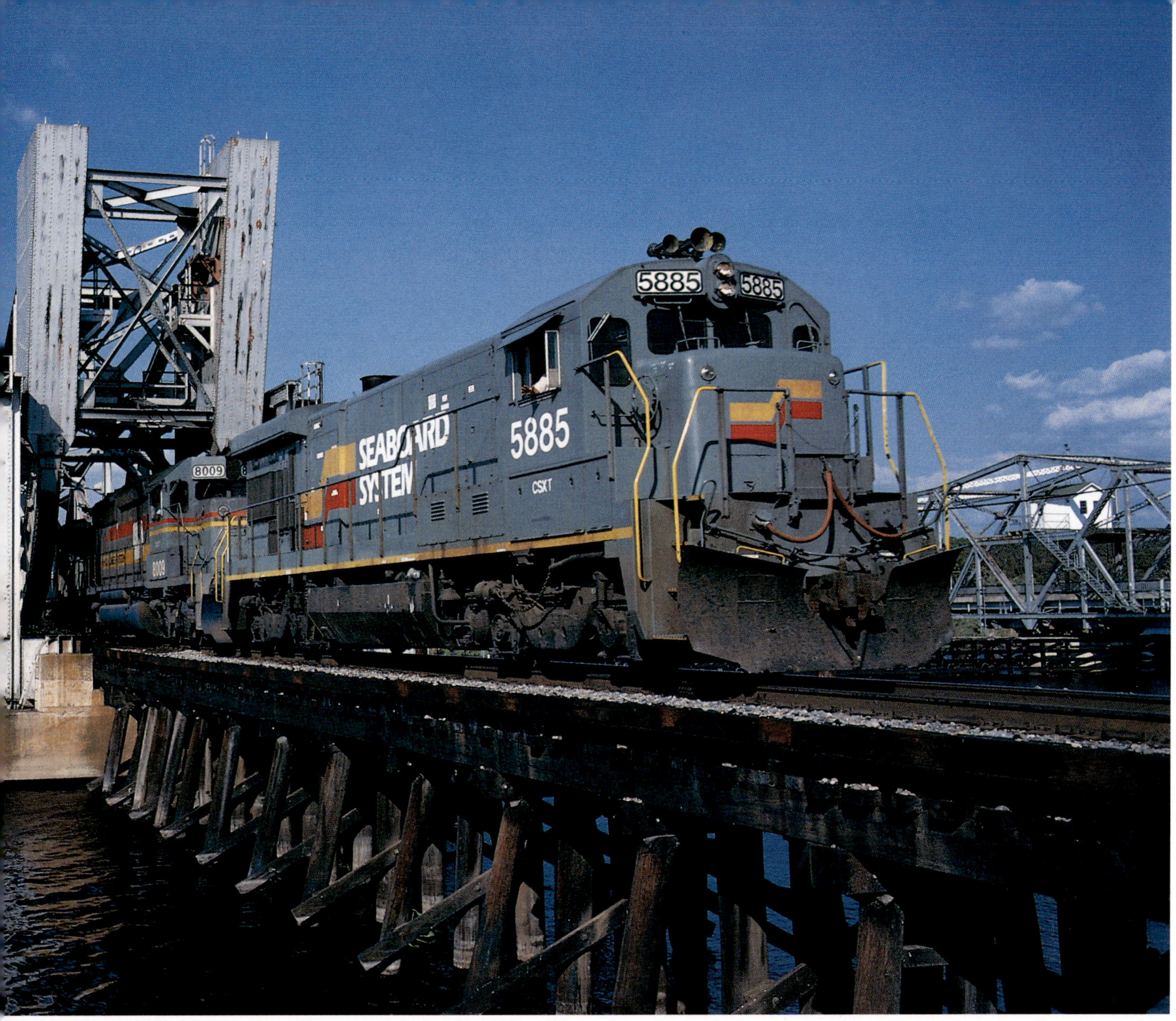
5885
5885
SEABOARD SYSTEM
5885
CSXT
8009

431
ARGIE
14

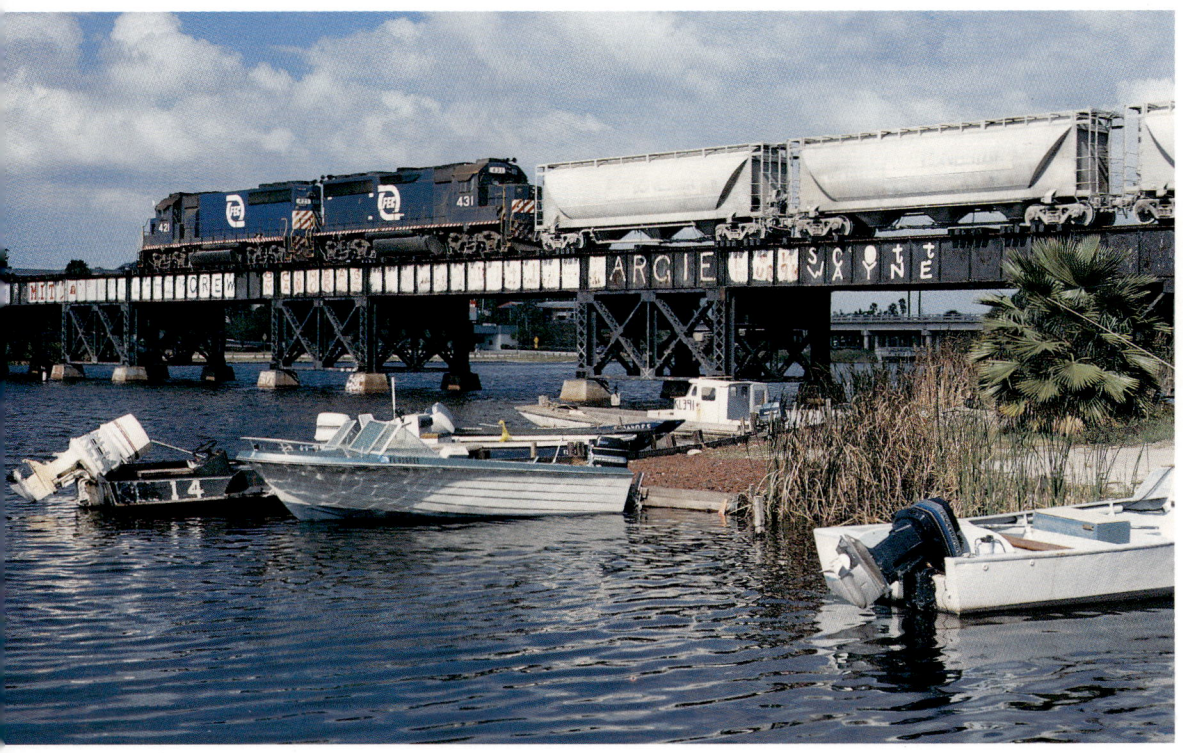

5858
5858

NORFOLK SOUTHERN
SOUTHERN
2433
3505
SOUTHERN
6633
6633

LEFT: Swinging through a curve at Emerson, Georgia, Seaboard System-dressed CSX GE B36-7 5858 ushers Sea-Land Double Stacks south toward Atlanta, March 7, 1987. This line is CSX's vital Knoxville-Atlanta main, which owns a heritage dating back to the Western & Atlantic and the Civil War's "great locomotive chase" involving the *General*. Photo: George W. Hamlin.

BELOW LEFT: Norfolk Southern's "Thoroughbred" image is apparent as NS SD60s roll past Peagram Shops in Atlanta, October 5, 1987. Photo: Steve Glischinski.

BELOW RIGHT: In June 1986, Atlanta's Inman Yard forms the backdrop as Norfolk Southern diesels — most in Southern Railway colors — take hold of a short string of coal hoppers. Photo: George W. Hamlin.

RIGHT: In a remarkable mix of new and old, veteran CSX cab and booster EMD F units pull the road's hot Detroit-Atlanta RoadRailer south through Covington, Kentucky (across the Ohio River south of Cincinnati), June 12, 1988. Photo: Bryan Rice. **BELOW:** On CSX's twisting, scenic Cincinnati-Louisville ex-L&N route, known as the "Shortline," EMD SD40 8337 leans into a curve southwest of Covington. Photo: Mike Danneman.

BELOW: Riding high over the Cumberland River at Burnside, Kentucky, a northbound Norfolk Southern manifest navigates NS's "Rat Hole" in September 1987. A rather unusual diesel lash-up, headed by an N&W EMD GP35, includes a rebuilt Geep and two GP38s. Photo: Steve Glischinski.

ABOVE: In August 1986, 307 miles of ex-Illinois Central trackage in Kentucky was transformed into a new regional, the Paducah & Louisville. GP35 2534, the first diesel to wear P&L's livery, draws northbound tonnage across the dam of Barkley Lake in western Kentucky, May 1, 1987. Photo: Gary W. Dolzall. ABOVE RIGHT: At Grand Rivers, Kentucky, on the P&L, the heritage of the line is recalled by three Illinois Central Gulf EMD SD40s delivering a unit train of Illinois coal for transloading into river barges on the nearby Tennessee River. Photo: Jerry Mart.

RIGHT: Against a sky building with a spring storm, Norfolk Southern SD60s hurry a Memphis-bound freight westward near Germantown, Tennessee, April 23, 1988. Photo: David M. Johnston.

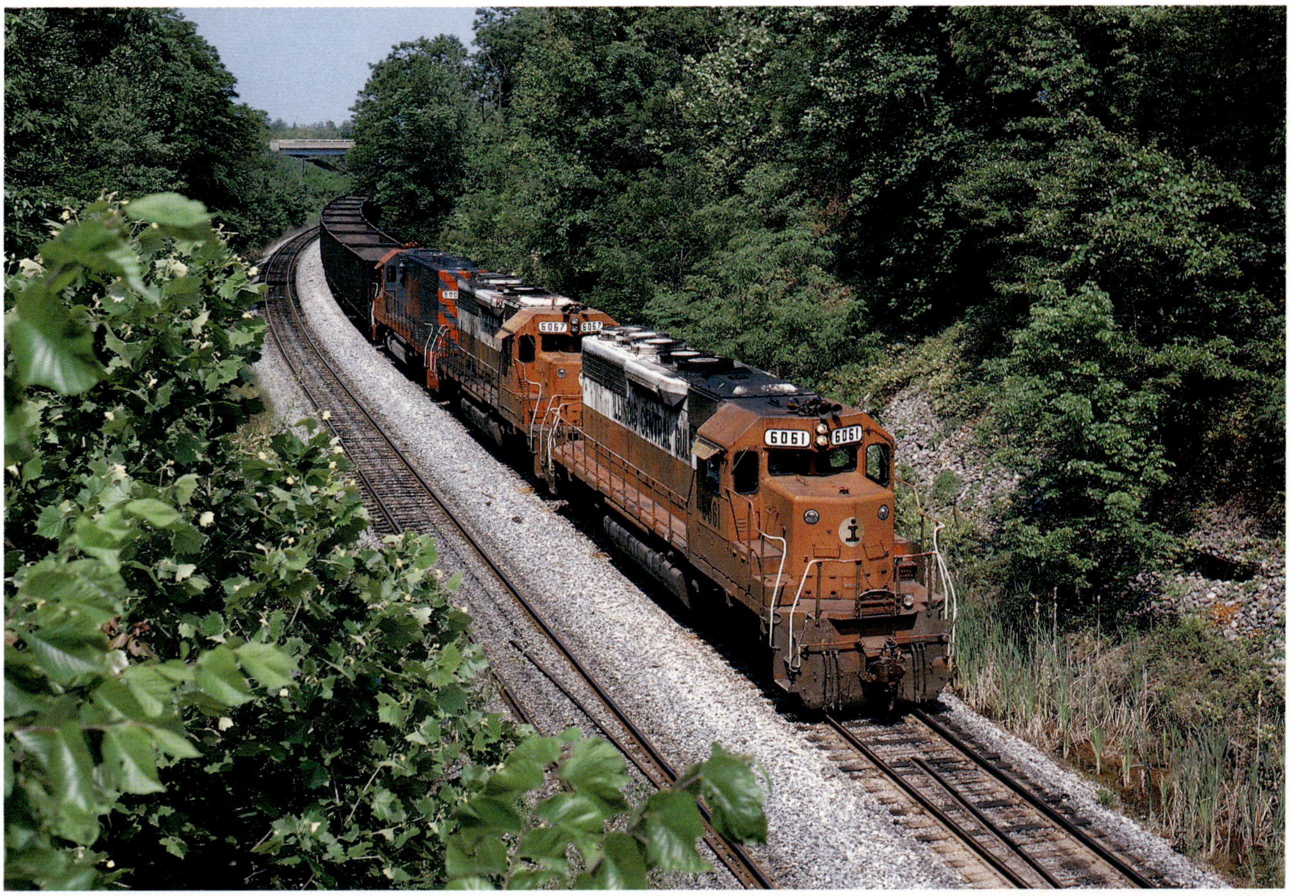
6061
6061

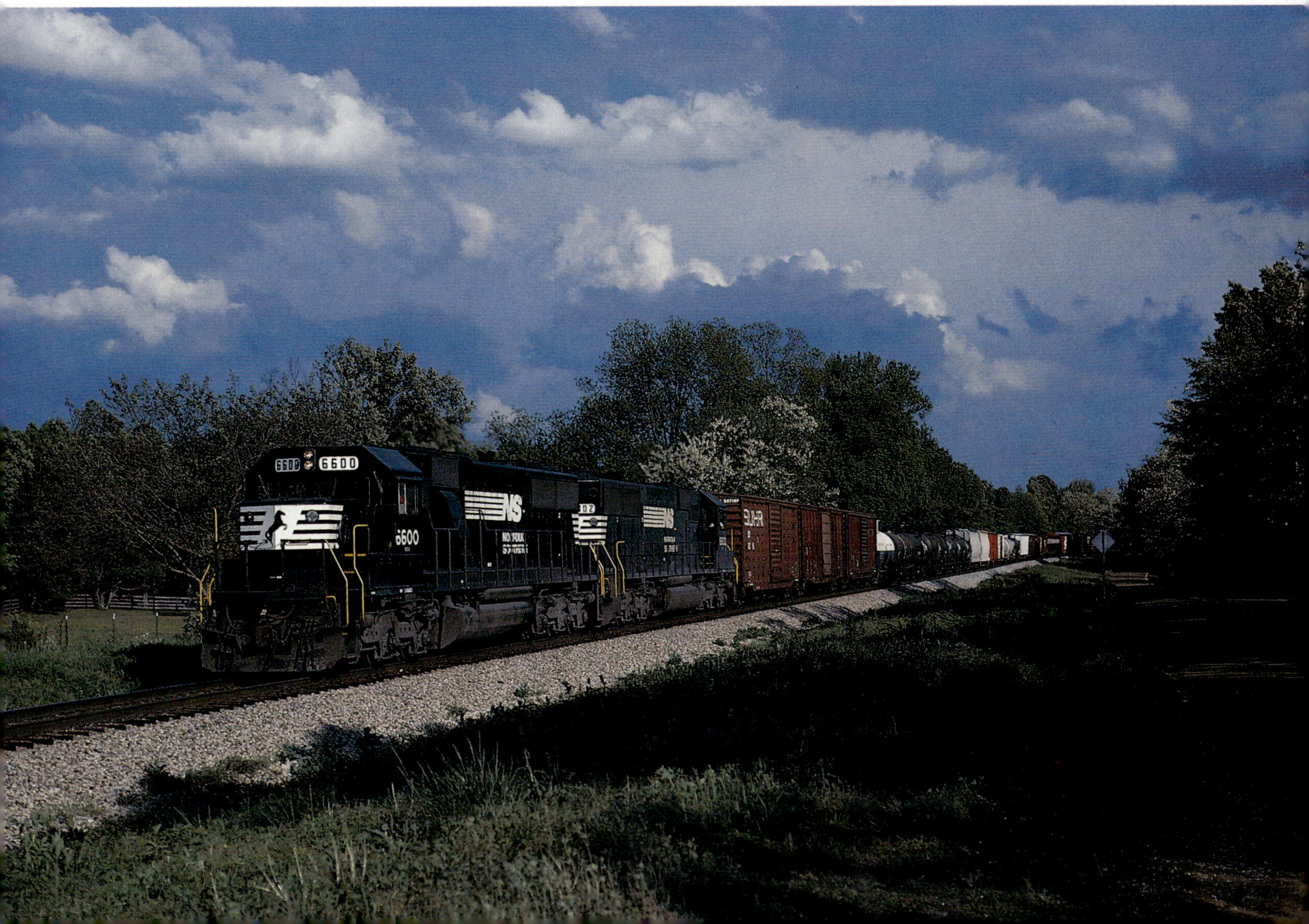
6600
6600
NS

About as short as short lines come, with two miles of track, the Old Augusta Railroad was opened in 1983 to haul forest products and paper from Augusta, Mississippi, to a connection with Illinois Central. Crossing the Leaf River on a modern concrete and steel trestle is the short line's complete roster, EMD GP7 669 and NW2 100. Photo: Louis Saillard.

Another Mississippi-based short line, the Meridian & Bigbee is older (formed in 1917) and longer (51 miles) than neighboring Old Augusta. On August 20, 1987, M&B 106, an ex-Santa Fe CF7 rebuild, and chop-nosed GP9 104 huddle at the road's home base, Meridian. Photo: Joe McMillan.

LEFT: A CSX freight vaults across the Locust Fork of the Warrior River near Trafford, Alabama, October 15, 1988. This is CSX's Nashville (Tennessee)-Birmingham line. Photo: Ron Flanary.

BELOW: On a February 1988 morning, Amtrak's eastbound *Crescent* rides the timbers of Norfolk Southern's Lake Ponchartrain trestle, northeast of New Orleans. Photo: Steve Glischinski. RIGHT: With its train trailing back across the Mississippi River toward Arkansas, Union Pacific EMD GP38-2 2243 makes a grand entrance into Memphis, Tennessee. Photo: David M. Johnston.

LEFT: Trundling toward New Orleans, 18 miles to the south, Kansas City Southern GP38-2s stroll above Bonnet Carre Spillway (between Lake Ponchartrain and the east bank of the Mississippi River), north of Norco, Louisiana, November 7, 1987. Photo: Louis Saillard.

4
RAILROADING'S MIDWESTERN MIXING POT

Where steel rails across America meet,
and a city claims title as America's railroad capital

AMERICA HAS OFTEN BEEN CALLED a melting pot, where peoples from around the world have come to live, mixing their rich histories and ethnic characteristics into a diverse yet singular society. In railroading terms, the industrial Upper Midwest is America's mixing pot.

In a region roughly bordered by the waters of the Great Lakes and the Ohio and Mississippi rivers — in the five states of Ohio, Indiana, Michigan, Illinois, and Wisconsin — the train-watcher can witness each of America's Super Seven freight railroads, plus a majority of this country's other Class 1s. And at the heart of the region, indeed, at the heart of American railroading itself, stands Chicago.

Chicago: It has for decades been labeled America's railroad capital, and while the megamerger era has somewhat blurred the rail divisions between north and south, east and west, Chicago still holds its claim. Of the Super Seven, only Southern Pacific does not send its rails into Chicago. Beyond the Super Seven, Class 1s Soo Line, Chicago & North Western, Grand Trunk, and Illinois Central are included in Chicago's railroad roll call.

LEFT: Against the skyline of America's railroad capital — Chicago — Burlington Northern E9s congregate for the evening commuter rush of September 10, 1987. Photo: Gary W. Dolzall.

The angular, ultra-modern lines of a Norfolk Southern C39-8 — the big GEs are sometimes called "satellites" — contrast to the surroundings of aging brick structures at Hammond, Indiana, east of Chicago. Norfolk Southern 8587 is riding NS's ex-Nickel Plate main line eastbound over the Indiana Harbor Belt crossing. Photo: Gary W. Dolzall.

A look at the route map in the center spread of an Amtrak timetable will show you that Chicago remains the crossroads for American intercity rail travel, too. Only in Chicago Union Station will a day's train-watching net visions of the *Broadway Limited* and *California Zephyr*, the *City of New Orleans* and *Empire Builder*. And beyond Amtrak, add Metra (Chicago's regional rail commuter authority), a commuter operation second in diversity only to that found in Gotham, a commuter operation featuring blue-and-red F40s, elegant E units still wearing Burlington Northern's green and white, and even double-deck, multiple-unit electrics.

For the train-watcher, it is a grand exercise, in person or simply on a map, to trace around Chicago following the path of one of the Windy City's belt railroads and consider all you encounter. Such a journey, say along the 114-mile Indiana Harbor Belt, offers a testament to Chicago's stature as America's rail capital.

The experience could begin anywhere in the Calu-

met region of Northwest Indiana, in Gary or Hammond or East Chicago, in a land still dominated by the old industrial age. Here, amid dusty red steel mills and aging brick buildings, the IHB first meets the eastern rail giants — CSX, Norfolk Southern, and Conrail. Indeed, for Conrail (which, with Soo Line, owns the Harbor Belt), IHB's double-track main is a major artery for moving eastern tonnage and intermodal traffic to and from the western railroads.

Across the Indiana-Illinois state line, the IHB intersects with more Class 1 railroads, from the east . . . and south . . . and west. At Dolton it crosses CSX and Union Pacific and slips under Illinois Central. At Blue Island crossing it meets the Grand Trunk. Then, as IHB turns northwest, the western giants begin to appear: first Santa Fe's busy double track at McCook, then Burlington Northern's triple-track main at Congress Park, then C&NW at Proviso, then parent Soo Line at Franklin Park (all this, not to mention IHB's connections or crossings with other than Class 1s, with regionals Chicago Central and

Silver, Japanese-designed electric cars of America's last interurban road — the 76-mile Chicago South Shore & South Bend — stand along the old wooden platforms of Chicago's Randolph Street Station on an October 1986 eve. Photo: Alex Mayes.

Having departed Illinois Central's Chicagoland freight terminal, Markham Yard, IC SD20 2005 (rebuilt by the railroad from an EMD SD24) leads a Memphis-bound freight past Metra electrics at Park Forest South, Illinois. The double-decker commuter electrics — called "Highliners" — operate on IC out of Randolph Street Station. Photo: Mike Danneman.

ABOVE: On December 3, 1988, at Union Pacific's Dolton intermodal terminal, UP SD60 6067 begins a Chicago-Dallas journey with a string of RoadRailers. UP acquired direct Chicago access — via the old Chicago & Eastern Illinois — when it merged with Missouri Pacific. BELOW: Drawing interchange from Chicago's northwest side toward Blue Island Yard, Indiana Harbor Belt SW1500s swing through LaGrange, Illinois, March 3, 1987. Both photos: Gary W. Dolzall.

McCook crossing: One of railroading's hotspots in Chicagoland is the McCook (Illinois) crossing of the joint IHB-B&OCT and Santa Fe's east-west main. ABOVE: Heading north, destined for Soo Line's Bensenville Yard, Grand Trunk Western GP40 6405 pounds through McCook at dusk, December 5, 1987. Photo: Gary W. Dolzall. LEFT: The Belt Railway of Chicago uses the IHB between BRC's huge Clearing Yard and Chicago & North Western's Proviso Yard. With a typical smoke eruption, southbound BRC Alco C424s accelerate through McCook, bound home on September 6, 1986. Photo: Mike Danneman.

Iowa Interstate and Chicago, Missouri & Western, with terminal roads like the Belt Railway and Baltimore & Ohio Chicago Terminal and Elgin, Joliet & Eastern).

As it traces from east to northwest, IHB ever more takes on the appearance of not only a belt line but also a Chicago freight freeway. While IHB or Conrail diesels lugging steel coil cars may suggest tradition, other IHB movements suggest the future. With the trains — and diesels — of C&NW and Soo and BRC and CSX and GT and Conrail all regularly trodding along its silvered path, IHB reveals a style of railroading that is increasingly time-sensitive, increasingly devoted as much to the trailers and containers that serve Northwest Chicago's light industries as to the gons and hoppers that serve Calumet's steel mills.

Arguably, the Indiana Harbor Belt (or the Belt Railway of Chicago or B&OCT, for that matter) offers a snapshot, a microcosm, of Chicagoland railroading. But there is more. There is the raw speed of the piggyback or Double Stack or RoadRailer trains that hustle in and out of town behind diesels dressed in the colors of Santa Fe or C&NW or NS or Conrail. There are the massive, pulsating freight yards named Corwith and Cicero and Clearing. There are the scenes that blend people and passenger trains — the bustle of Chicago Union Station, the lingering terminals at LaSalle and Randolph streets, the spider webs of trackage

Chicago & North Western blankets the northwest side of Chicagoland with busy rail lines. RIGHT: On C&NW's high-density Chicago-Nebraska main line, a westbound *Falcon* piggyback behind GP50 5074 curls through downtown Elmhurst, Illinois, just west of Proviso Yard, March 5, 1988. Photo: Gary W. Dolzall. BELOW: On C&NW's route between Chicago and Milwaukee, Wisconsin, Metra commuters operate as far north as Kenosha, Wisconsin. At Waukegan, Illinois, Metra F40s sleep away the cold night of December 5, 1987. Photo: Mike Danneman/Gary W. Dolzall.

that glisten under the skyline of Chicago's Loop and point Amtrak and commuter trains toward their far-flung destinations, and the handsome suburban stations that dot the mains of BN and C&NW and Soo Line.

Because Chicago is so captivating, so awesome, it is comfortable to become preoccupied with the Windy City. And yet to do so at the expense of the rest of the Midwest is to miss so much worthy of attention. There await in the region other cities alive with railroading. There is the Queen City of Cincinnati and her quiltwork of trackage that melds railroading's

north and south. And there are Indianapolis, Milwaukee, Columbus, Cleveland, Toledo, and Detroit.

Yes, there is urban intrigue, and there is also Midwestern rural beauty, an out-in-the-country railroad drama. For the train-watcher, there await the experiences of blue-and-yellow Santa Fe diesels snarling up Illinois' Edelstein Hill, and Burlington Northern pig trains slicing along the east bank of the Mississippi. There await the experiences of Upper Michigan's remote pine country being awakened by the march of a slogging iron ore train, and of Conrail hotshot van trains jabbing across northern Indiana and Ohio

Earning its nickname — "the race track" — Burlington Northern's famous three-track main line west from Chicago to Aurora, Illinois, hosts a sprint race at Highlands, July 2, 1988, between a westbound Burlington Northern commuter behind E9 9903 and Amtrak's F40PH-powered *California Zephyr*. So far, it's a dead heat. Photo: Gary W. Dolzall.

bound toward Toledo and Cleveland. There await the intrigue of GT or NS or CR or CSX diesels hustling autos and auto parts west and south from the Motor City, and of Amtrak's *Empire Builder* swirling along the fabled path of the old Milwaukee Road across Wisconsin. The Midwest suggests IC coal trains wading into the hills of Southern Illinois, Southern Pacific and UP diesels climbing toward the great bridge over the Mississippi at Thebes, and Norfolk Southern and CSX and Conrail trains venturing through the farmlands and rugged hills of central and southern Ohio, Indiana, and Illinois, bound toward St. Louis.

The Midwest is a land of big-time railroading — of the Super Seven and middleweight Class 1s, of Amtrak and Metra. It is a territory of spunky regionals (Wisconsin Central and Chicago Central, for instance), of short lines and belt lines and branch lines, even of America's last remaining interurban (the 76-mile Chicago South Shore & South Bend). And it is, most certainly, a land for the train-watcher.

Ohio rails. ABOVE: With a Cincinnati departure behind, a Norfolk Southern freight led by a GE C36-7 and EMD SD40 rolls on CSX track at Hamilton, May 2, 1986. Soon, the NS train will regain home rails and head northwest toward Ft. Wayne, Indiana. Photo: Bryan Rice. BELOW: On CSX's ex-Baltimore & Ohio main between Deshler, Ohio, and Pittsburgh, Chessie GP40s hustle an eastbound pig train through Ravenna. Photo: Steven Cigolle. BELOW LEFT: Famous Terminal Tower is visible in the background as Norfolk & Western J-class 4-8-4 611 brings the glory of steam railroading to Cleveland, August 3, 1986. Photo: Ron Cady.

ABOVE: The Kalamazoo River reflects the images of a CSX Chicago-Grand Rapids freight treading the old Pere Marquette at New Richmond, Michigan, October 10, 1986. Photo: Paul H. Dalman. BELOW: Detroit & Mackinac Alco C425 1280 drives a freight through fresh snow at Topinabee, Michigan, January 1988. D&M operates more than 400 miles in Michigan. Photo: Ron Cady.

On Indiana's own railroad — the Monon — street running was something of a tradition, and the practice continues to this day on CSX, witness this southbound freight wandering through the town square of Bedford, Indiana, April 29, 1986. Photo: Reid McNaught.

RIGHT: Only two hours remain in the journey of Amtrak's New York-Chicago *Lake Shore Limited* as F40PH 361 guides the streamliner through Hudson Lake, Indiana, September 10, 1988, on Conrail's ex-NYC main. Photo: Mike Danneman.

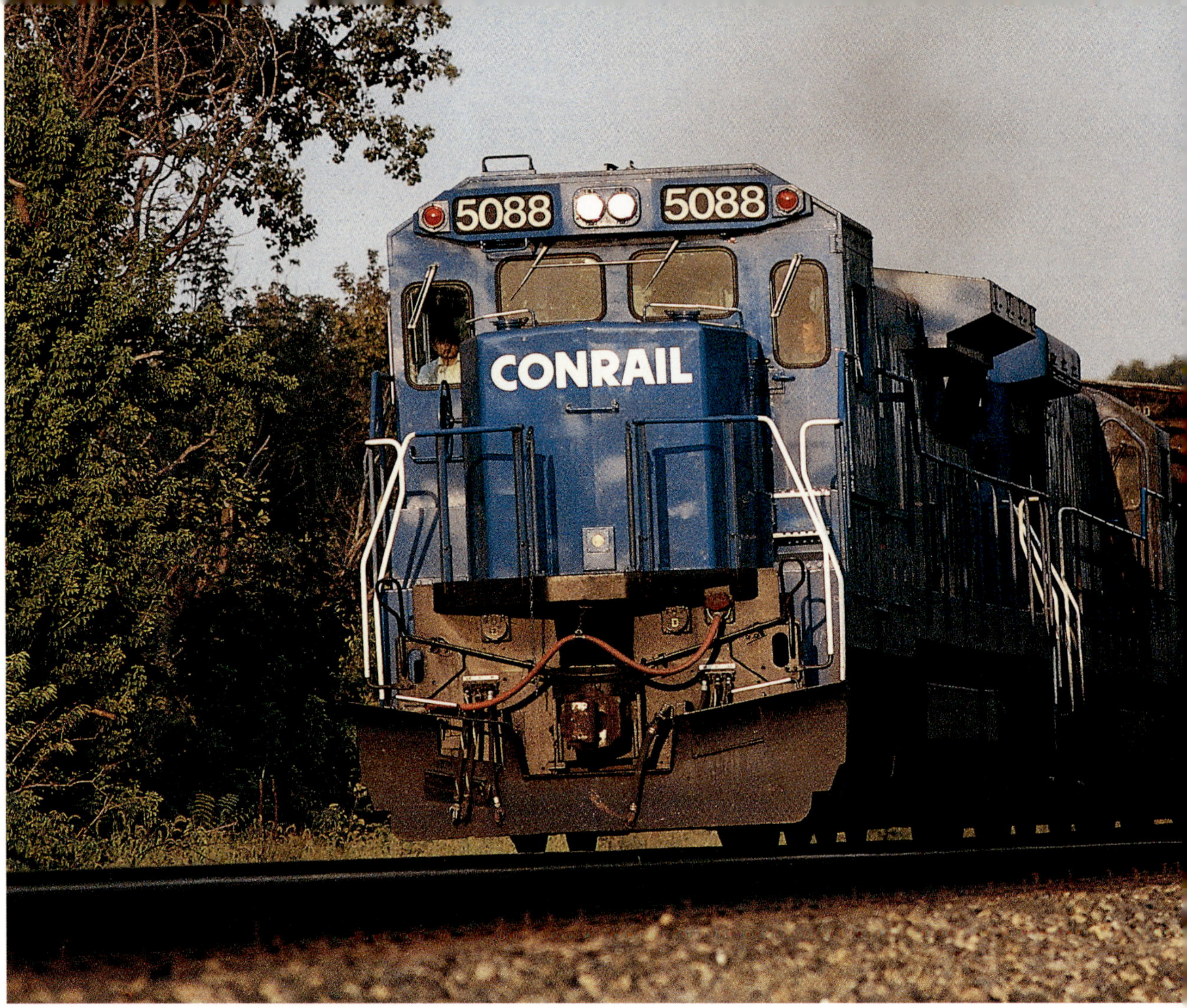
5088
5088
CONRAIL

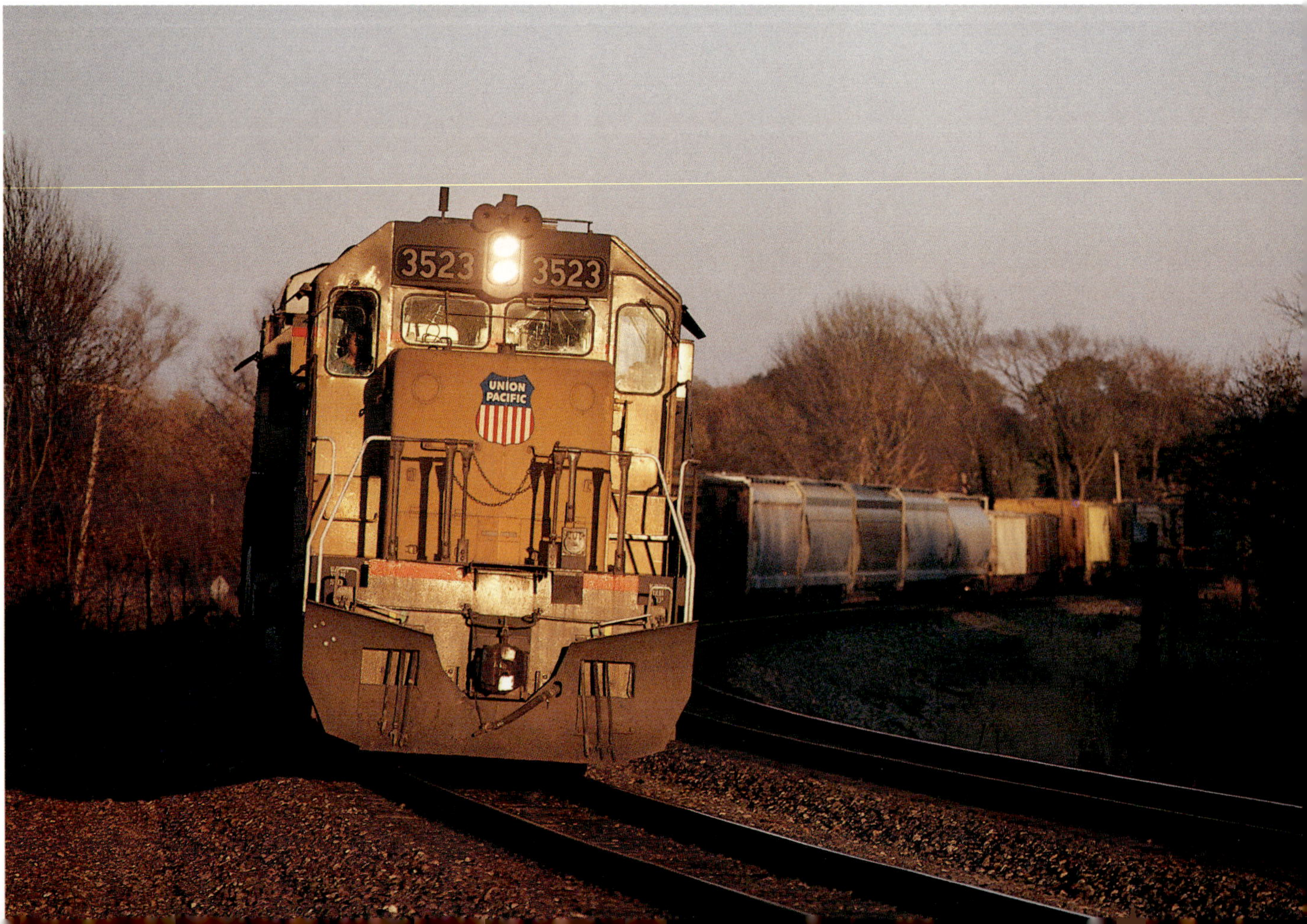
3523
3523
UNION PACIFIC

One of the most tonnage-intense routes in the U. S. is Conrail's ex-New York Central main line across northern Indiana and Ohio. ABOVE LEFT: In September 1988 at New Carlisle, Indiana, new Conrail Dash 8-40B 5088 and a GE sister sling tonnage westbound toward Chicago. Photo: Mike Danneman. BELOW: At 7:50 a.m., on a foggy September 1988 morning, Conrail GP40-2s clip through New Carlisle with an eastbound intermodal. Photo: Gary W. Dolzall. BELOW LEFT: Run-through power from the west is common on Conrail's main as far east as Elkhart, Indiana. At dusk, October 30, 1988, Union Pacific SD40-2 3523 heads a westbound Conrail freight near Otis, Indiana. Photo: Gary W. Dolzall.

PRECEDING PAGES: Into the mid-1980s, Michigan's Upper Peninsula drew train-watchers with the promise of six-axle Alco diesels hauling ore on two roads — Chicago & North Western and the Lake Superior & Ishpeming. On North Western's ore line running west from Escanaba, a trio of Alco C628s stand under a twilight sky at Little Lake, October 18, 1986. Alas, by the end of 1986, C&NW's Alcos were stored. Photo: Gary W. Dolzall/Mike Danneman.

LEFT: On Upper Michigan's other ore-hauling Alco road, the 60-mile Lake Superior & Ishpeming, bright red ex-Santa Fe Alco RSD15s usher 120 empty ore cars across Dead River Trestle, heading back from the docks at Marquette to Eagle Mills for more loads, August 10, 1988. Photo: Scott Hartley.

ABOVE: Alcos in Wisconsin. The 255-mile Green Bay & Western long has been a bastion of Alco diesel power, making possible scenes such as C424s 319 and 321 (both ex-Conrail units) guiding GB&W train 1 west into the sunset at Arnott, June 2, 1985. Photo: Scott Hartley.

RIGHT: On Soo Line's ex-Milwaukee Road main line across Wisconsin, Amtrak's eastbound *Empire Builder* glides toward Tunnel City, shortly to plunge into the railroad bore that gave the community its name. Photo: Mike Danneman. FAR RIGHT: Sandwiched between the Mississippi River and towering bluffs, tiny Alma, Wisconsin, plays host to a Burlington Northern freight headed north toward the Twin Cities, July 23, 1988. Photo: Gary W. Dolzall

RIGHT: On a wintery eve along what was once the "Route of the 400," Chicago & North Western SD45 963 works a freight near Sussex, Wisconsin. ABOVE: Sunset silhouettes a northbound freight, powered by two C&NW SD40-2s and a leased Duluth, Missabe & Iron Range SD9, on frigid January 2, 1989. The train is at Campbellsport, Wisconsin, on the ex-C&NW Butler (Wisconsin)-Green Bay line, now part of the regional Fox River Valley Railroad. Both photos: Gary W. Dolzall.

Symbolic of the birth of America's largest regional is this night scene of Wisconsin Central GP38 4007 and Soo Line Geep 4228 at Waukesha, Wisconsin, December 26, 1987. Nearly 2000 miles long, WC was formed from ex-Soo trackage in October 1987. Photo: Mike Danneman/Gary W. Dolzall.

ABOVE: Ex-Milwaukee Road SD40-2s, quickly relettered for new owner Soo Line, grind west from Milwaukee, Wisconsin, on September 12, 1987, trailing an unbroken string of covered hoppers. Photo: Gary W. Dolzall. BELOW: A few miles farther west on the old Milwaukee Road double-track main line, Amtrak's Superliner-equipped *Empire Builder* runs wrong main to slide past tonnage headed by Soo Line GP30 716, July 26, 1987. Photo: Mike Danneman.

ABOVE: A pair of ex-Burlington Northern SD45s, one repainted in Wisconsin Central livery, roll WC train 12 through marsh country near Theresa, Wisconsin, in December 1988. Prior to the Soo Line-Milwaukee Road merger and subsequent formation of Wisconsin Central, this line was part of Soo's main artery between Chicago and the Twin Cities. Photo: Gary W. Dolzall.

BELOW: Veiled in the fury of a brutal snowstorm, December 15, 1987, Soo Line SD60 6015 struggles west through Brookfield, Wisconsin, on the Soo's ex-Milwaukee Road Chicago-Twin Cities route. Photo: Mike Danneman.

Grandeur of the Mississippi River country: North of Savanna, Illinois, in a panorama view from Mississippi Palisades State Park, Burlington Northern EMD GP50 3151 scurries toward Chicago with an *Expediter* intermodal train from the Twin Cities. Photo: Mike Danneman.

RIGHT: Autumn colors dress the bluffs along the Mississippi near Savanna, Illinois, as Burlington Northern SD40-2 7877 and a sister head east with an intermodal train, October 15, 1988. Photo: Gary W. Dolzall.

BELOW: Since her restoration to life in 1979 by the Ft. Wayne (Indiana) Railroad Historical Society, Nickel Plate Berkshire 765 has served as a mainstay on excursion passenger trains in the Midwest and East. Visiting Chicago & North Western rails in September 1984, the beautiful NKP 2-8-4 whistles her way through Rochelle, Illinois, at sunset. Photo: Joe McMillan.

Green-diamond logos affixed to Chicago Central GP20 981 recall the Illinois Central origins of the 777-mile regional road formed in 1985, mostly from IC's old Iowa Division. CCP 981 and sisters, all Milwaukee Road veterans, stand against a twilight sky at Freeport, Illinois. Photo: Mike Danneman.

PRECEDING PAGES: From Chicago southwest across rural Illinois, Santa Fe stretches its busy double-track main line toward Kansas City and beyond. East of Chillicothe, Illinois, Santa Fe GE and EMD diesels point a Chicago-bound piggyback train across AT&SF's 1,696-foot-long bridge over the Illinois River. Photo: Mike Danneman.

ABOVE: With a string of tank cars behind, Santa Fe GE U23B 6337 leads train 102 west out of the yard at Chillicothe, Illinois, May 18, 1985. **ABOVE RIGHT:** West of Chillicothe, Santa Fe's main climbs Edelstein Hill on a 1.1 percent grade. At renowned Houlihan's Curve, August 20, 1988, Santa Fe FP45 5990 leads a westbound auto rack train. Both photos: Mike Danneman.

BELOW LEFT: Near Media, Illinois, Amtrak's Los Angeles-Chicago *Southwest Chief* scurries over Media Trestle on the Santa Fe, May 31, 1986. Photo: Mike Danneman. BELOW: Santa Fe bridges the Mississippi River at Ft. Madison, Iowa. On May 22, 1988, AT&SF SD45-2 5805 tugs an eastbound intermodal train across the Mississippi and into Illinois. Photo: Gary W. Dolzall.

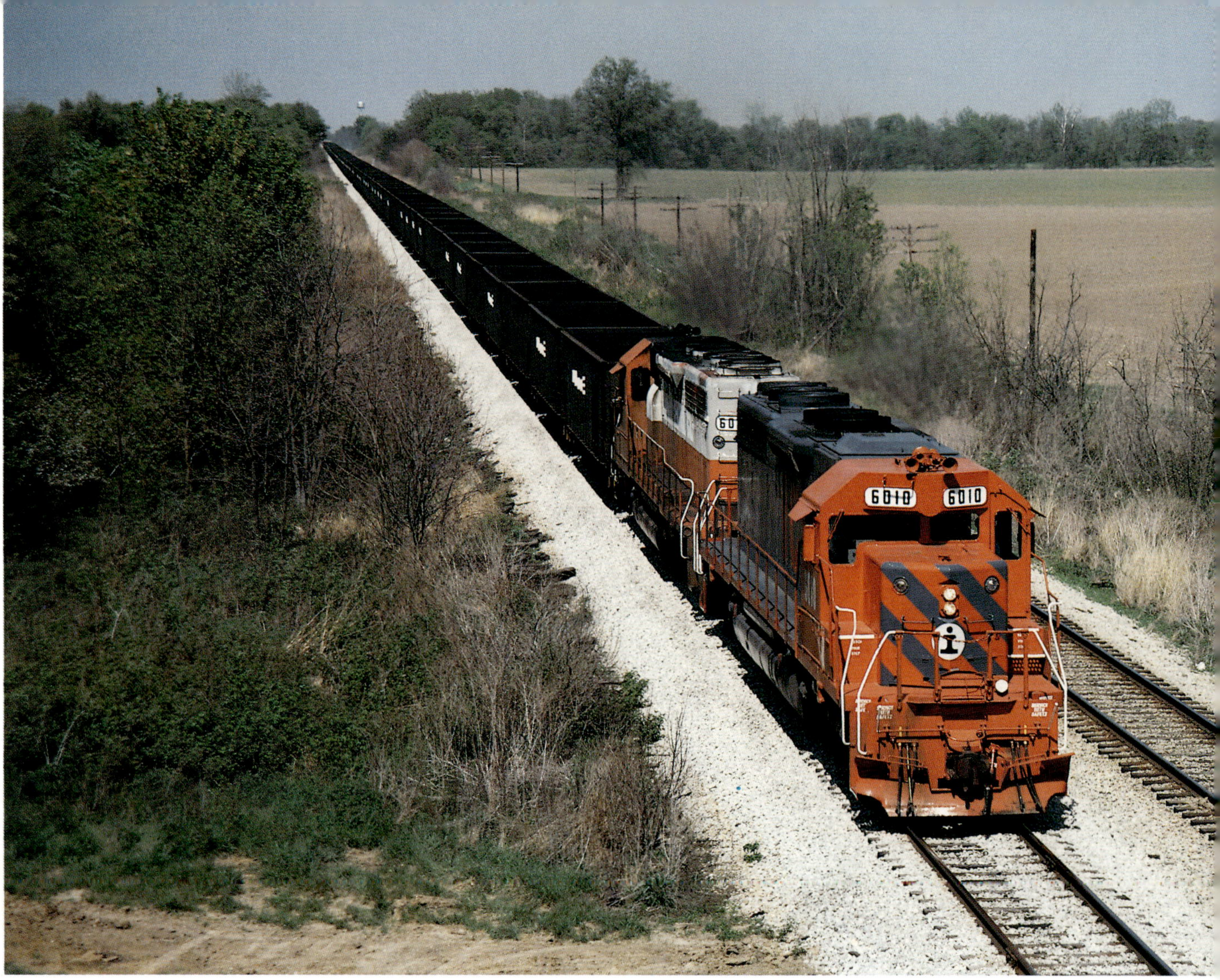
6010
6010

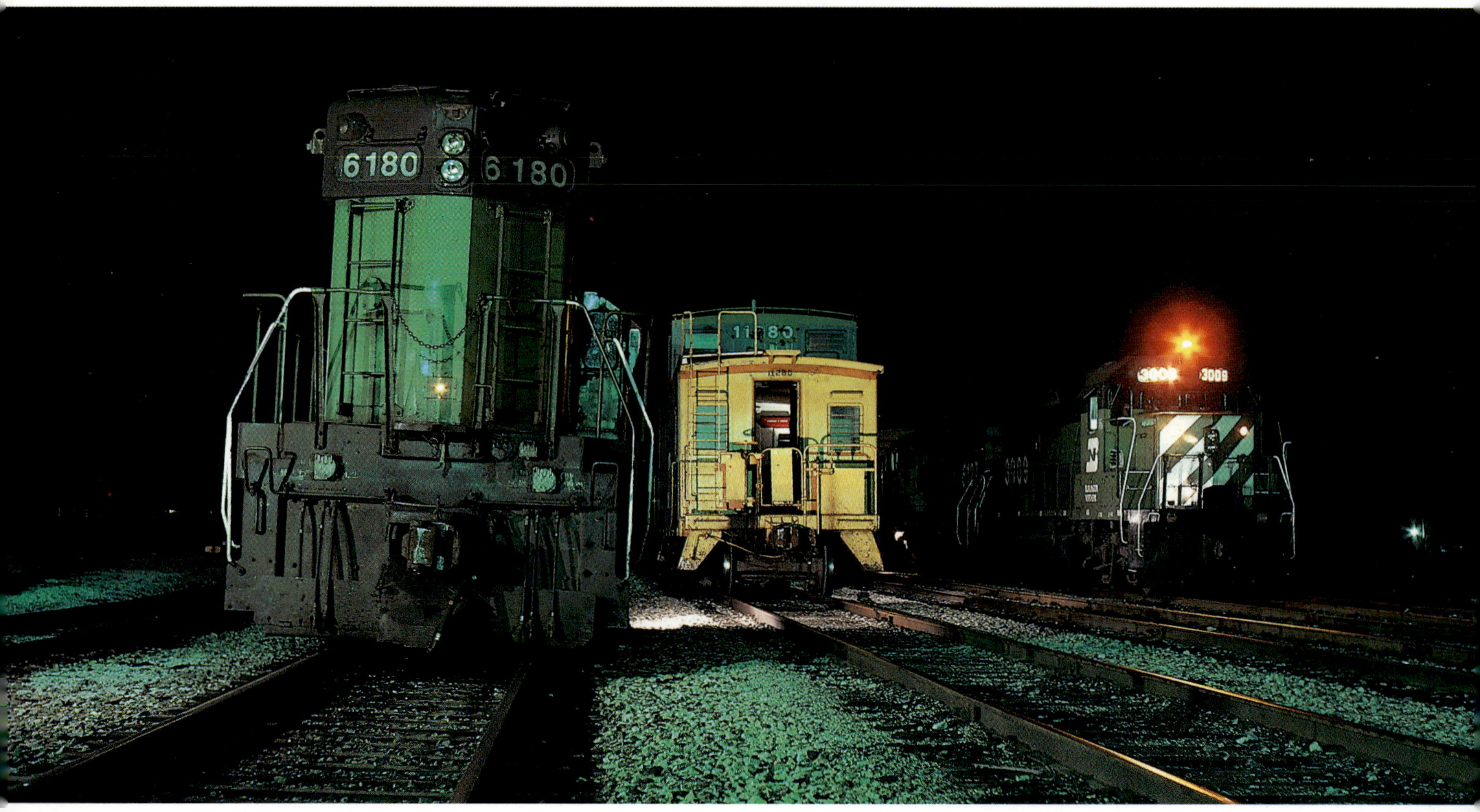
6180
6180

LEFT: Empty coal hoppers follow SD40A 6010 and a sister down Illinois Central's main, near Alma in southern Illinois. The big SD wears a fresh coat of the final orange-and-gray scheme applied by Illinois Central Gulf, before IC returned to its traditional name — and black paint. Photo: Gary W. Dolzall.

Bound from Kansas City to St. Louis, a Chicago, Missouri & Western freight trundles through Jerseyville, Illinois, October 26, 1988. Motive power is ex-Western Pacific GP40s; trackage is ex-Illinois Central Gulf (and before that, Gulf, Mobile & Ohio). The regional CM&W is largely a reincarnation of GM&O-predecessor Alton between Chicago, St. Louis, and Kansas City. Photo: Paul H. Dalman.

LEFT: At Centralia, Illinois, Burlington Northern power congregates on a September 1984 night. On ex-CB&Q rails, Burlington Northern reaches into southern Illinois to tap coal sources and even reaches Paducah, Kentucky, to interchange with the regional Paducah & Louisville. Photo: Mike Danneman.

5
RAILROADING IN THE HEARTLAND

In the great middle of this nation,
endless and endearing railroading discoveries

AMONG ALL THE GRAND train-watching venues across America, there are select locations, even entire regions, that have gained extraordinary fame. The Northeast Corridor, Horse Shoe Curve, the Front Range of the Rockies, Southern California's Cajon Pass and Tehachapi Loop — all have become renowned by their sheer drama, and, in certain cases, by their relative proximity to population.

Train-watchers have always been attracted to the concentrated brand of railroading found in the Northeast, to the diversity of Chicago and the Midwest, to the unbridled vigor and majesty of big-time railroading in the far West. Which is to suggest that the South, and America's middle Heartland, while by no means ignored by train-watchers, remain the most open for investigation, the most ripe for discovery. Indeed, in the great mass of America stretching westward from the Mississippi River toward the Rockies, from the Gulf of Mexico to the Canadian plains, endless and endearing new railroading experiences await the modern train-watcher.

LEFT: The drama of railroading in the Heartland is revealed as Union Pacific diesels roll eastbound under an inspiring sky at North Platte, Nebraska, June 1983. Photo: Mike Danneman.

RIGHT: Red River Valley & Western CF7s arrive at Wahpeton Jct., North Dakota, against endless plains, with an eastbound grain train, June 21, 1988. The regional RRV&W was formed in 1987 to work 667 miles of ex-Burlington Northern (mostly ex-Northern Pacific) branch lines in North Dakota. Photo: J. David Ingles.

If there is a single image of railroading most often associated with America's middle, it is that of the great transcons — UP, BN, SP, and AT&SF — hustling long strings of tonnage across vast flatlands. Union Pacific's ribbons of steel across Nebraska and the railroad's link eastward through Iowa with C&NW is a pure embodiment of such drama. Tracing along a path shared by old U. S. Highway 30, this great steel conveyor stretches through Nebraska towns named North Platte and Kearney and Grand Island, through Iowa communities christened Carroll and Nevada and Cedar Rapids. In the modern age, it bulges and pulses with tonnage, with C&NW/UP *Falcon* piggybacks, with gargantuan Double Stack trains, with black-snake unit coal trains pouring out of Wyoming's Powder River Basin toward the industrial Midwest, and with grain trains carrying the harvest of the Heartland's fields.

The UP/C&NW main line is, generally, one that meets expectation — slingshot straight stretches, long and arcing curves, gentle wanderings along the North Platte River. And yet, as proof positive that the Heartland offers the unexpected, the remarkable discovery, one need only venture a few miles west of Boone, Iowa, to the rim of the Des Moines River valley. There, on steel girders 186 feet over the river below, C&NW's rails cross the Des Moines River atop one of the great railway structures in this land — the Kate Shelley bridge. Such is the intrigue of the

Heartland — the expected, randomly mixed with the extraordinary.

If the UP/C&NW east-west main is the premier example of big-time, fast-paced mainline railroading set in granger territory, its claim is only fractionally stronger than that of similar lines belonging to other of railroading's Super Seven. Santa Fe's east-west main line, after crossing the Mississippi River, snips Iowa, curls through central Missouri to reach Kansas City, then stretches its legs across the Kansas plains. And AT&SF is alive with traffic. Ditto the other mains that stretch across mid-America — Southern Pacific's ex-Rock Island Golden State Route slicing southwest from St. Louis and Kansas City toward El Paso; SP's Sunset Route stretching east-west along the lower rim of America on its New Orleans-Houston-Los Angeles route; Burlington Northern's mains toward Denver and the Wyoming coalfields, its throbbing far-north artery spun from the Twin Cities across Minnesota, North Dakota, and Montana to the Pacific Northwest; the routes of Santa Fe and SP and BN and UP (ex-Missouri Pacific and ex-Katy) that link the Midwest with Texas, Gulf ports, and Mexico. And along virtually all these routes, as with C&NW's Kate Shelley bridge, the remarkable or the unanticipated awaits — the curling, rolling, remote route of the Santa Fe through Northern Missouri; BN's Wendover Canyon looming out of the plains of eastern Wyoming; the bleak, moonlike terrain of the cen-

A Dakota, Minnesota & Eastern freight curls westward through pure granger territory at Blunt, South Dakota, June 22, 1988. Leading the charge is SD10 551 (a rebuilt SD9), still in the colors of its prior owner, Milwaukee Road. Created in 1986, 965-mile regional road DM&E operates primarily on ex-Chicago & North Western rails. Photo: J. David Ingles.

tral Dakota plains; the rock-strewn high deserts sliced by Southern Pacific in West Texas; and so much more.

As late as the 1960s railroading and coal were synonymous with the East and South, with Chessie and Norfolk & Western and Clinchfield. But no longer, as Burlington Northern and C&NW/UP extract millions of tons of bituminous from Wyoming's plains, and punch much of it eastward across the Heartland. Which, yet again, draws us to the surprising nature of this territory. There are probably few states in this land more associated with a flat granger landscape than Nebraska, but in the northwest corner of the state, on BN's coal-heavy Alliance Division main,

Lake Superior ore country! RIGHT: On 73-mile Erie Mining, a road that totes taconite ore from Hoyt Lakes to Taconite Harbor, Minnesota, three EMD F9s and a GP38 guide 100 ore cars out of 1,800-foot Cramer Tunnel in September 1988. Photo: Steve Glischinski. BELOW: At Saunders, Wisconsin, near the twin ports of Superior, Wisconsin, and Duluth, Minnesota, trains of Chicago & North Western, Duluth, Winnipeg & Pacific, and Duluth, Missabe & Iron Range draw together on October 20, 1985. Photo: Mike Danneman. BELOW RIGHT: Maroon diesels of the most famous of Lake Superior's iron ore carriers — 357-mile Duluth, Missabe & Iron Range — drag empty ore cars westward at Biwabik, Minnesota. Photo: J. David Ingles.

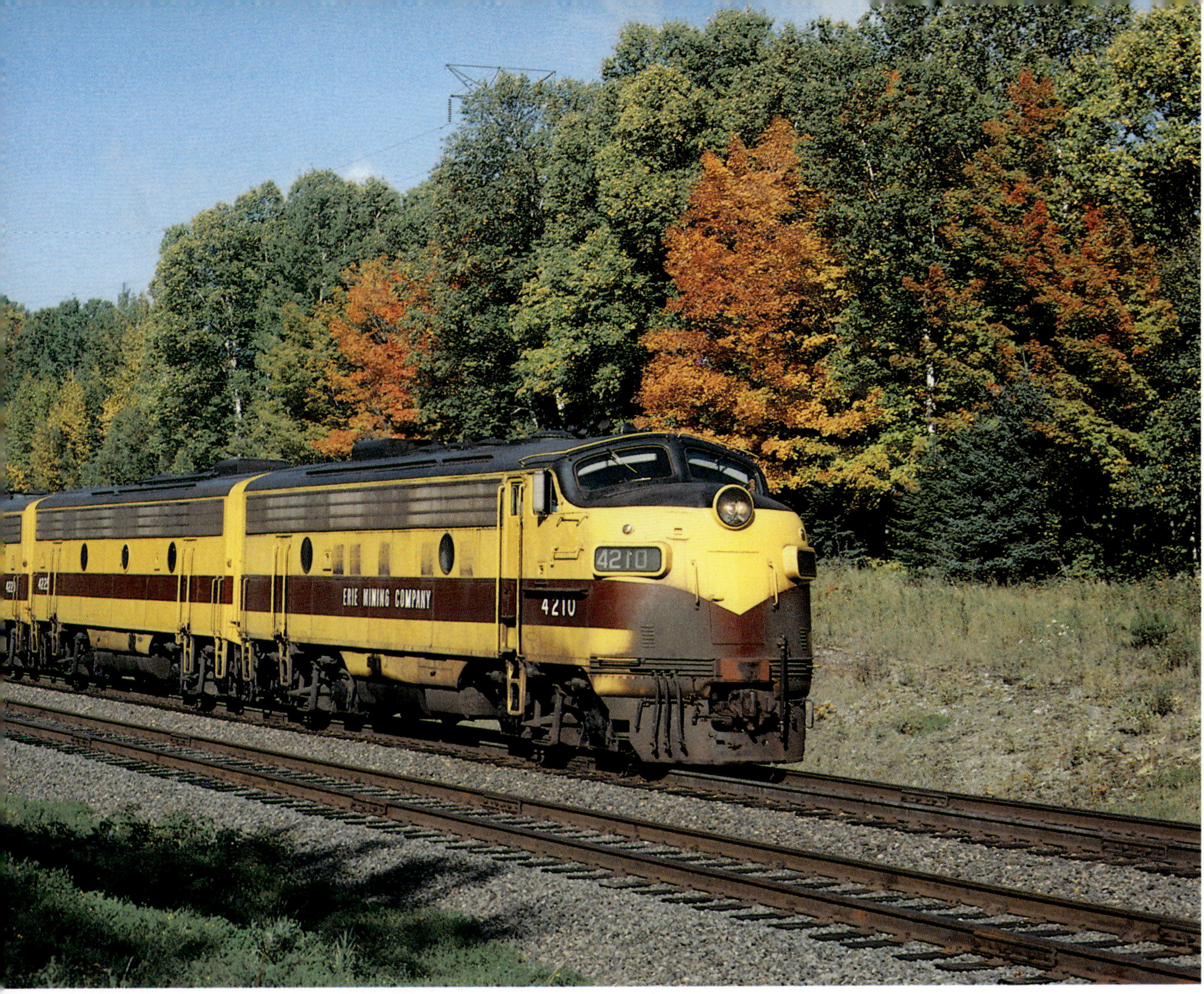
4210
ERIE MINING COMPANY
4210

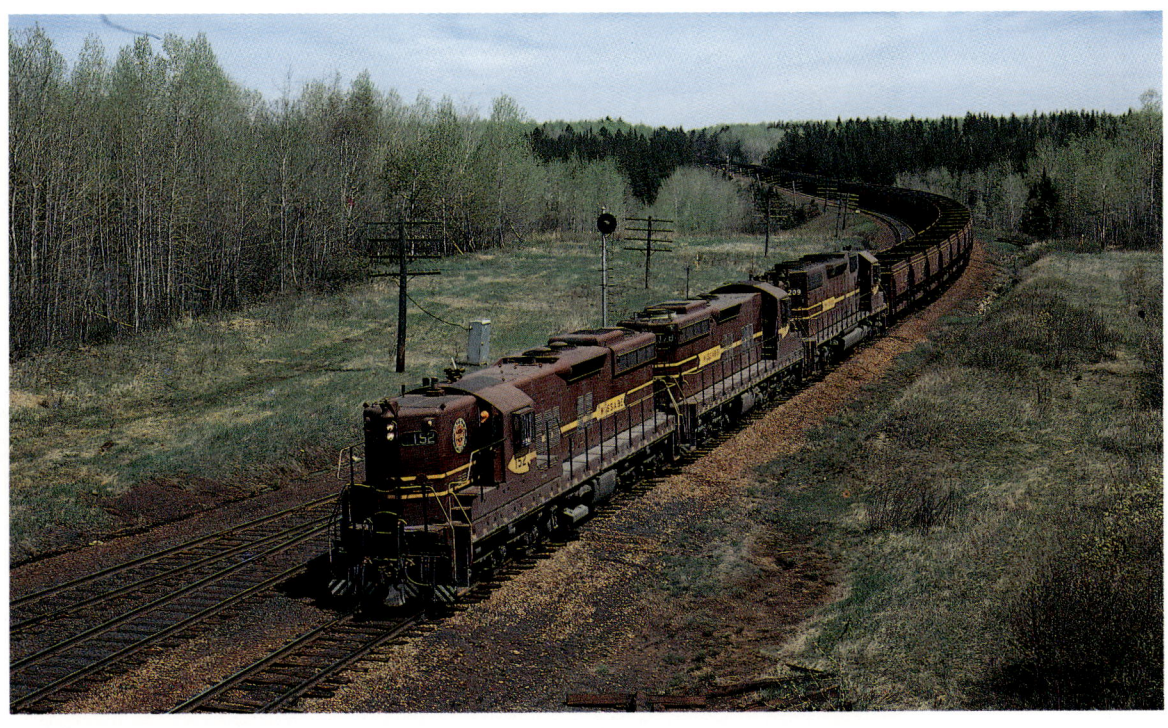

ABOVE: Snug against Mississippi River bluffs at St. Paul, Minnesota, Burlington Northern SD40-2 7033 and an *Expediter* intermodal train scurry past Soo Line SD40-2 6381 and a grain train, stopped for a crew change, July 23, 1988. Photo: Gary W. Dolzall. RIGHT: Soo Line SD40-2s hustle a *Sprint* train along the west bank of the Mississippi in southeastern Minnesota, February 18, 1987. Photo: Steve Glischinski.

awaits Crawford Hill. There the train-watcher will discover BN battling Windy Point and Crawford Horseshoe, using all the muscle of eight or more burly diesels placed fore and aft to lift 14,000-ton coal trains over twisting 2 percent grades.

As elsewhere, middle America's out-in-the-country railroad drama is spliced together by its cities, by the communities where ribbons of steel touch and intertwine. In America's middle the list of great railroad cities reads St. Louis and Kansas City and Omaha, Dallas and Fort Worth and Houston, Minneapolis and St. Paul. Often, these cities — St. Louis and Kansas City, in particular — mark the far westward reaches of the eastern rail giants, of Conrail and CSX tapping St. Louis and Norfolk Southern attaining Kansas City. While Chicago remains railroading's crossroads, the megamerger era has ever softened the distinction between east and west.

Not unlike the Northeast, where the formation of Conrail so changed the rail map, America's Heartland in the last decade has been remolded by the hand of necessity. Changes came in the form of the 1980 demise of the Rock Island and 1980-1982 retrenchments of the Milwaukee Road; the merger of the Milwaukee into Soo Line; UP's acquisition first of Missouri Pacific, then of Katy; and in the mileage trimmings of C&NW and BN and Illinois Central. From this boiling caldron of change came abandonments, renewals (D&RGW's arrival in Kansas City via ex-MP trackage rights from Pueblo, and SP's acquisition of the old Rock's Golden State Route the most notable), and new regionals to serve middle America — Chicago Central (ex-ICG) and Iowa Interstate (ex-Rock), Arkansas & Missouri (ex-BN), and Dakota, Minnesota & Eastern (ex-C&NW) among the most prominent.

In short, America's Heartland offers all the intrigue of modern railroading — the colossal operations of Super Seven roads like BN and AT&SF and UP; the individualistic, comfortable styles of middleweight Class 1s such as Soo Line and Kansas City Southern; the wanderings of granger regionals like Iowa Interstate and Dakota, Minnesota & Eastern. The heart of America reveals railroading in a myriad of forms, from a Duluth, Missabe & Iron Range train tugging 10,000 tons of iron ore toward Lake Superior docks to Amtrak's *Southwest Chief* slicing across the plains of Kansas at 90 mph, from a diminutive short line named Louisiana & Delta tugging covered hoppers through bayou country to Norfolk Southern racing RoadRailers toward Kansas City. Which all suggests that America's Heartland deserves a good, close look from train-watchers.

PRECEDING PAGES: Striding across the Des Moines River valley atop the 186-foot-high spires of the Kate Shelley bridge west of Boone, Iowa, Chicago & North Western and Union Pacific diesels power a westbound Double Stack train on September 17, 1988. Photo: Mark Danneman.

ABOVE: Chicago & North Western SD50 7019 heads an eastbound priority freight along Chicago & North Western's traffic-dense Chicago-Nebraska main line, near Wheatland, Iowa, April 9, 1988. BELOW: From the ashes of the old Rock Island across Iowa and Illinois, the 590-mile regional Iowa Interstate was formed in 1984. At Iowa City, IAIS EMD Geeps 400 and 414 — the latter still in Illinois Central Gulf colors — congregate at dusk, April 8, 1988. Both photos: Gary W. Dolzall.

A late-running Amtrak eastbound *California Zephyr* burrows deep in a cut below the rolling hills of eastern Nebraska as it nears the Missouri River at Plattsmouth, riding Burlington Northern's Denver-Chicago main line, October 4, 1987. Photo: Steve Glischinski.

On the Overland Route across Nebraska. ABOVE: Although the power of this westbound hopper train belongs to Chicago & North Western, the rails are those of Union Pacific's traditional Overland Route. Pacing along old U. S. Highway 30, SD60 8035 is at Maxwell, heading for North Platte. ABOVE RIGHT: East of North Platte, UP GE C30-7s glide along Nebraska's grasslands. RIGHT: Dusk at Birdwood, west of North Platte, silhouettes UP SD40-2s. Three photos: Mike Danneman.

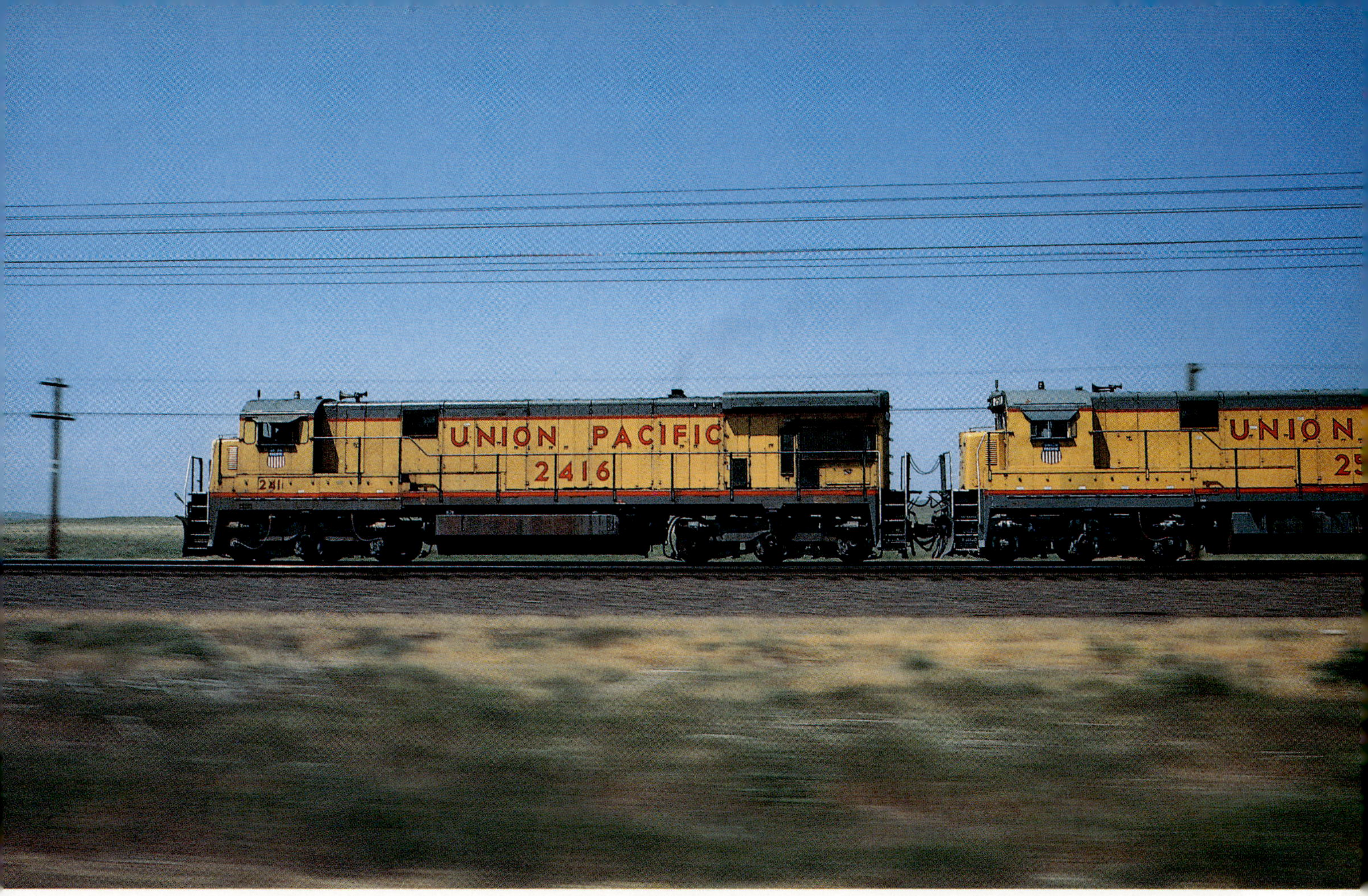
UNION PACIFIC
2416
UNION

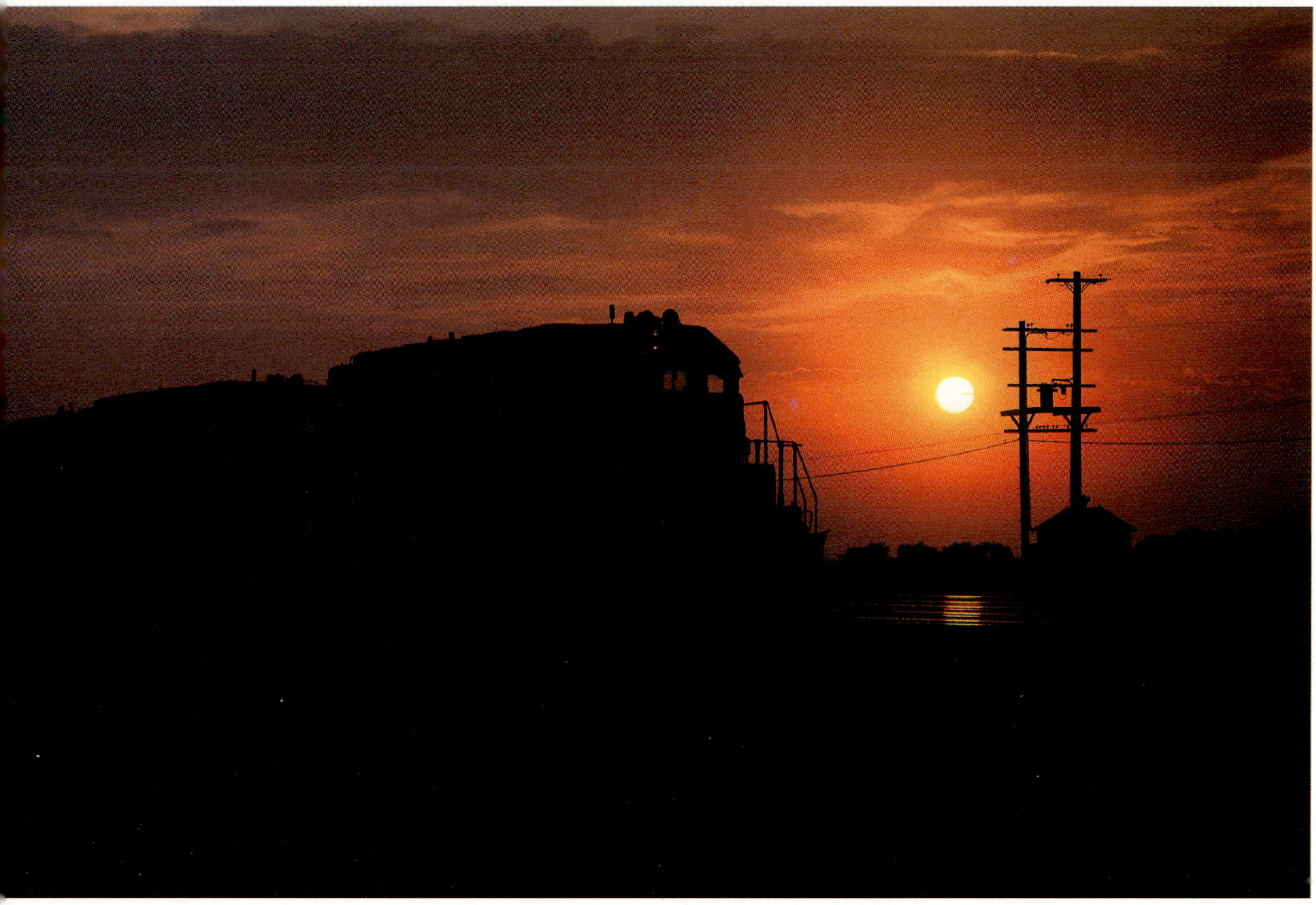

Burlington Northern's Crawford Hill: Day in, day out, coal trains claw over Crawford Hill on BN's Alliance Division in northwestern Nebraska. ABOVE: Coal loads are drawn around the horseshoe at Rutland, Nebraska, June 19, 1988. Photo: Steve Patterson. LEFT: A quintet of GEs leads hoppers along Crawford's double track on July 4, 1988. Once a single-track route of the old Burlington, this line was heavily rebuilt and modernized in the 1980s to handle BN's enormous Powder River Basin coal traffic. Photo: Mike Danneman.

ABOVE: An unexpected scenic delight of the old Burlington, and now of Burlington Northern, is Wendover Canyon in southeast Wyoming. Curling along the North Platte River, BN EMD and GE diesels draw a hopper train north toward the Powder River Basin in the summer of 1985. Photo: Tom Danneman. BELOW: At Guernsey, Wyoming, BN diesels — with the help of a UP SD40-2 — draw UP hoppers across the North Platte River. Photo: Mike Danneman.

The plains of eastern Colorado are home to 128-mile Great Western Railway, a road that makes its living hauling agricultural products. At Hardman, May 22, 1987, GP9 211 issues a plume of exhaust smoke as it totes tank cars filled with corn syrup. Photo: Ron Flanary.

Near Ensign, Kansas, an aging EMD duo of GP30 and GP35 provide ample motive power for a local's five cars and caboose treading Santa Fe's Kansas Division branch line between Dodge City, Kansas, and Boise City, Oklahoma, September 5, 1986. Photo: Dave Gayer.

Argentine Yard, on the west side of Kansas City, is a vital point on Santa Fe's Chicago-West Coast main line. Santa Fe F45 5960 is tended inside AT&SF's three-track Argentine diesel servicing facility, March 10, 1989. In a typical month, Santa Fe pumps more than 4 million gallons of fuel into its diesels at this location alone. Photo: Gary W. Dolzall.

LEFT: Curling through the maze of Kansas City Terminal trackage, Katy EMD GP39-2 379 heads a westbound empty hopper train on cold December 8, 1985. The trailing units are another Katy Geep (purchased from Conrail and still in CR blue), and a trio of Burlington Northern GEs. Photo: Mike Danneman.

BELOW: At sunset, an SD40-2 still in Milwaukee Road's orange-and-black livery draws a Chicago-bound Soo Line freight through Sheffield crossing, on the east side of Kansas City. Soo Line attained Kansas City with its 1985 purchase of Milwaukee Road. Photo: Mike Danneman.

ABOVE: A Chicago-bound Santa Fe piggyback curls eastward, May 16, 1987, amid the remote, rolling hills of northeastern Missouri near Baring. AT&SF typically dispatches 30 or more trains a day across this busy railroad. Photo: Mike Danneman. BELOW: It's Santa Fe's main line near Argyle, Iowa, but it looks more like Conrail as trains meet in May 1987. Conrail run-through power regularly operates on AT&SF as far west as Kansas City. Photo: Gary W. Dolzall.

Union Pacific GP38-2 2385, still wearing the blue livery of Missouri Pacific, teams with a sister already repainted in UP colors to power a local through Castlewood, Missouri, October 30, 1987. This route is the ex-Missouri Pacific main between Kansas City and St. Louis, now part of UP and utilized via trackage rights by Southern Pacific (Cotton Belt). Photo: Paul H. Dalman.

RIGHT: Busch Stadium, home of the St. Louis Cardinals major league baseball team, and the St. Louis arch are visible in the background as a Southern Pacific EMD SD45T-2 and GE B30-7 lug Double Stacks along the east bank of the Mississippi River in East St. Louis, September 13, 1986. Photo: Paul H. Dalman.

En route from Texas (with through car service from Los Angeles) to Chicago behind a pair of F40PH diesels, Amtrak's *Eagle* twists its way out of downtown St. Louis, Missouri, approaching the Eads Bridge over the Mississippi River. Since this May 31, 1986, photo was taken, the train has been renamed the *Texas Eagle*. Photo: Paul H. Dalman.

Restored to service in 1988 after nearly three decades of slumber in the National Museum of Transport at St. Louis, Frisco 4-8-2 1522 (built by Baldwin in 1926) quickly drew the admiration of train-watchers with her stylish lines and cracking exhaust. On October 22, 1988, the 4-8-2 heads out of St. Louis with an excursion train bound for Decatur, Illinois. Photo: Paul H. Dalman.

Cutting through the Ouachita Mountains of southwest Arkansas, Kansas City Southern train 82 calls at Blue Cut, Arkansas, May 29, 1982, en route from Shreveport, Louisiana, to Kansas City. Like SD40X 703, all motive power on 1,600-mile KCS is GM-built. Photo: David M. Johnston.

Arkansas & Missouri is a 145-mile regional created in 1986 to operate ex-Burlington Northern (Frisco) trackage between Monett, Missouri, and Fort Smith, Arkansas. A&M immediately drew the attention of train-watchers by equipping itself with Alco motive power, witness C420 44, RS32 42, and C420 46 emerging on October 24, 1987 from 1,700-foot-long Winslow Tunnel in northwest Arkansas. Photo: David M. Johnston.

Another smallish railroad famous for its motive power — in this case elderly EMD F units — is 61-mile Louisiana & North West, which extends from a Southern Pacific (Cotton Belt) connection at McNeil, Arkansas, to a link with MidSouth at Gibsland, Louisiana. Near Magnolia, Arkansas, L&NW F7 46 heads south with a freight that reveals one of the tonnage staples of the short line — pulpwood. Photo: Joe McMillan.

Since its origin in 1986 as a 403-mile regional spinoff of Illinois Central Gulf, the MidSouth has expanded to more than 1,200 miles and may soon qualify for Class 1 status. Along MidSouth's original east-west route, three Geeps draw a freight from Vicksburg, Mississippi, toward Monroe, Louisiana, across eastern Louisiana on March 16, 1988. Photo: J. Parker Lamb.

157

Santa Fe's preferred route for freight traffic west from Kansas City across the Heartland is via Wellington, Kansas, and Amarillo, Texas. ABOVE: West of the Cimarron River at Belva in northwestern Oklahoma, Santa Fe GE B23-7 6353 heads a mix of freight and intermodal tonnage, August 8, 1987. BELOW: At Amarillo in August 1985, Santa Fe westbound intermodal 288 eases up to East Tower behind GE U36C 8773 and three EMD diesels. Both photos: Joe McMillan.

No fewer than five trains are visible at Santa Fe's modern locomotive servicing facility at Temple, Texas, May 23, 1987, on AT&SF's main line between Fort Worth and Houston. Third from the left is an empty hopper train, bound back toward Wyoming's Powder River Basin, with mixed Burlington Northern and Santa Fe motive power. Photo: Reid McNaught.

Southwest of Austin, Texas, at Buda, Union Pacific GE and EMD diesels stroll southward on April 22, 1987, following the steel path of UP's ex-Missouri Pacific line which reaches to Laredo, Texas, and the Mexican border. Photo: Steve Glischinski.

PRECEDING PAGES: The ultra-modern skyline of Houston, Texas, contrasts with the lines of Katy GP7s 121 and 103, veterans constructed by Electro-Motive more than a quarter-century prior to this May 23, 1988, scene. Before the end of 1988, Katy was merged into Union Pacific and the Geeps were slated for retirement. Photo: Reid McNaught.

En route from Los Angeles to Houston and New Orleans, Southern Pacific's famous Sunset Route encounters the spell-binding gorges, canyons, and high desert country of West Texas. ABOVE: Five EMD diesels snake a freight through rocky Paisano Pass, November 30, 1986. Photo: Reid McNaught. ABOVE RIGHT: A quartet of GE B39-8s jumps across Eagle's Nest Canyon, February 13, 1988. Photo: Reid McNaught. BELOW RIGHT: Near Longfellow, Texas, at 10:55 a.m., December 10, 1981, the high desert pulses to the sounds of twin GE P30CH diesels hurrying Amtrak train 1 — the *Sunset Limited* — westward toward Los Angeles. Photo: Gary A. Rich.

6
RAILROADING IN THE WEST

Where the immensity and grandeur of the continent give stage to railroading glory

THE GREAT AMERICAN WEST: It is arguable that nowhere in this country, indeed, nowhere on this planet, is there a more appropriate stage for big-time, modern railroading. In spirit, the West and railroading share much — both are big, tough, demanding, both inspire, both awe the mind and dare the human imagination.

From the Rockies west to the shores of the Pacific, railroading occupies a land which at once gives it unbridled reign and ultimate challenge. The West offers railroads room to spin countless miles across grasslands and deserts, yet throws before them formidable barriers — the Rockies, the Sierra Nevada, the Cascades.

Appropriately, the great West is a land of great railroads. As the South is dominated by two of the Super Seven (NS and CSX), the West is today the domain of four giants — Union Pacific, Southern Pacific Lines, Santa Fe, and Burlington Northern. That three of those railroad names date virtually to the beginning of railroading in the West is testament to the strength and longevity of western-style railroading. And even Burlington Northern, although not formed until 1970, was envisioned as early as the 1890s by Great Northern's remarkable founder, James J. Hill.

LEFT: Dawn light greets Union Pacific Extra 3632 East as it exits Tunnel 6 on UP's historic Overland Route near Castle Rock, Utah, June 10, 1988. Photo: Blair Kooistra.

If American railroading is in fact a captivating mixture of tradition and transition, the West is proof positive. Second only to the Southern Railway and successor Norfolk Southern, the Union Pacific has rejoiced in its traditions of steam by firing up an elegant 4-8-4 and a potent 4-6-6-4 (UP 8444 and 3985) to retell the story of steam railroading. And on special occasions, Southern Pacific has welcomed to its rails a famous 4-8-4 wearing the numerals "4449." Yet, while the roll call of the Western rail giants remains much the same as it was when the likes of 8444 and 4449 saw daily service, the rules of Western railroading have been changed forever — witness UP's merger of Western Pacific, giving itself a direct link to California's Bay Area (and allowing UP to abandon its age-old alliance with SP's Overland Route); witness diminutive Rio Grande taking over giant SP, then folding itself (as an operating subsidiary, ala SP's Cotton Belt) into a new, stronger "Southern Pacific Lines," with D&RGW serving as a new SP direct line

LEFT: On Santa Fe's tonnage-heavy Belen Cutoff, AT&SF Richmond (California)-to-Chicago hotshot intermodal train 981 curls through Sais, New Mexico, at the west end of Abo Canyon, December 9, 1981. Santa Fe completed the Belen Cutoff across eastern New Mexico between Belen and Clovis in 1908 to allow its freights an alternate path to the treacherous 3 percent grades of Raton Pass. Photo: Gary A. Rich.

east across the Rockies toward the Heartland and the Midwest.

D&RGW — fabled Rio Grande — is a paradox of Western railroading: In a realm of railroad titans, such a modest property (1,848 route-miles before its expansion to Kansas City and marriage with SP) represents the embodiment of Western railroading's can-do spirit. That D&RGW should finally disappear as an independent entity only by its own hand, by folding itself into one of the Western giants, should come

as no surprise. The railroad born of the dreams of William Jackson Palmer in 1870, then strengthened by assumption of David Moffat's Denver & Salt Lake and the opening of the Dotsero Cutoff, forever defied the odds — and forever intrigued the train-watcher.

Rio Grande dared assault the Rockies head-on, with Big Ten Curve and numbered tunnels almost too numerous to count, with 6.2-mile-long Moffat Tunnel, with careful tracings of canyons named Glenwood and Ruby, with a run across the Utah desert and a

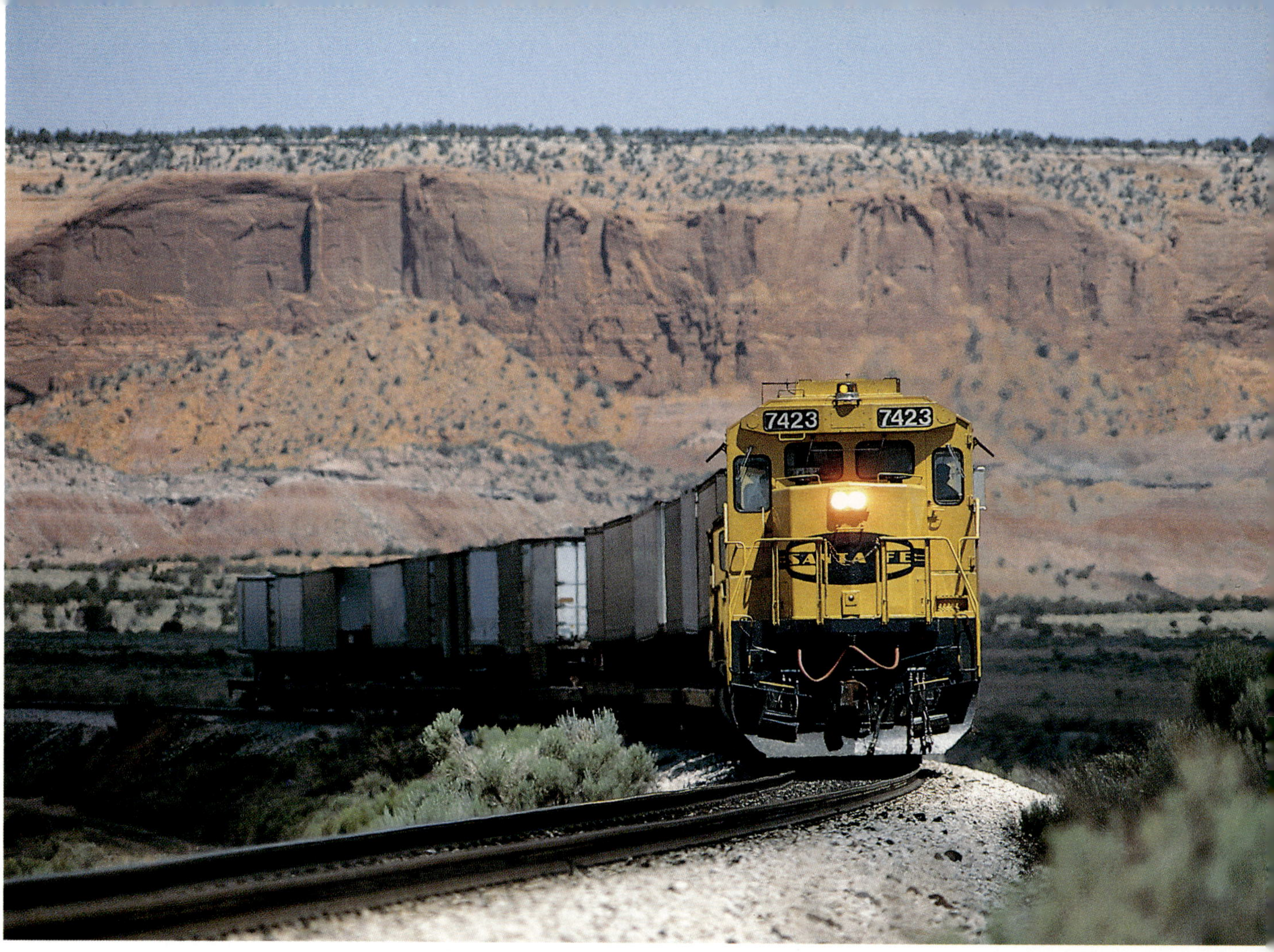
7423
7423
SANTA FE

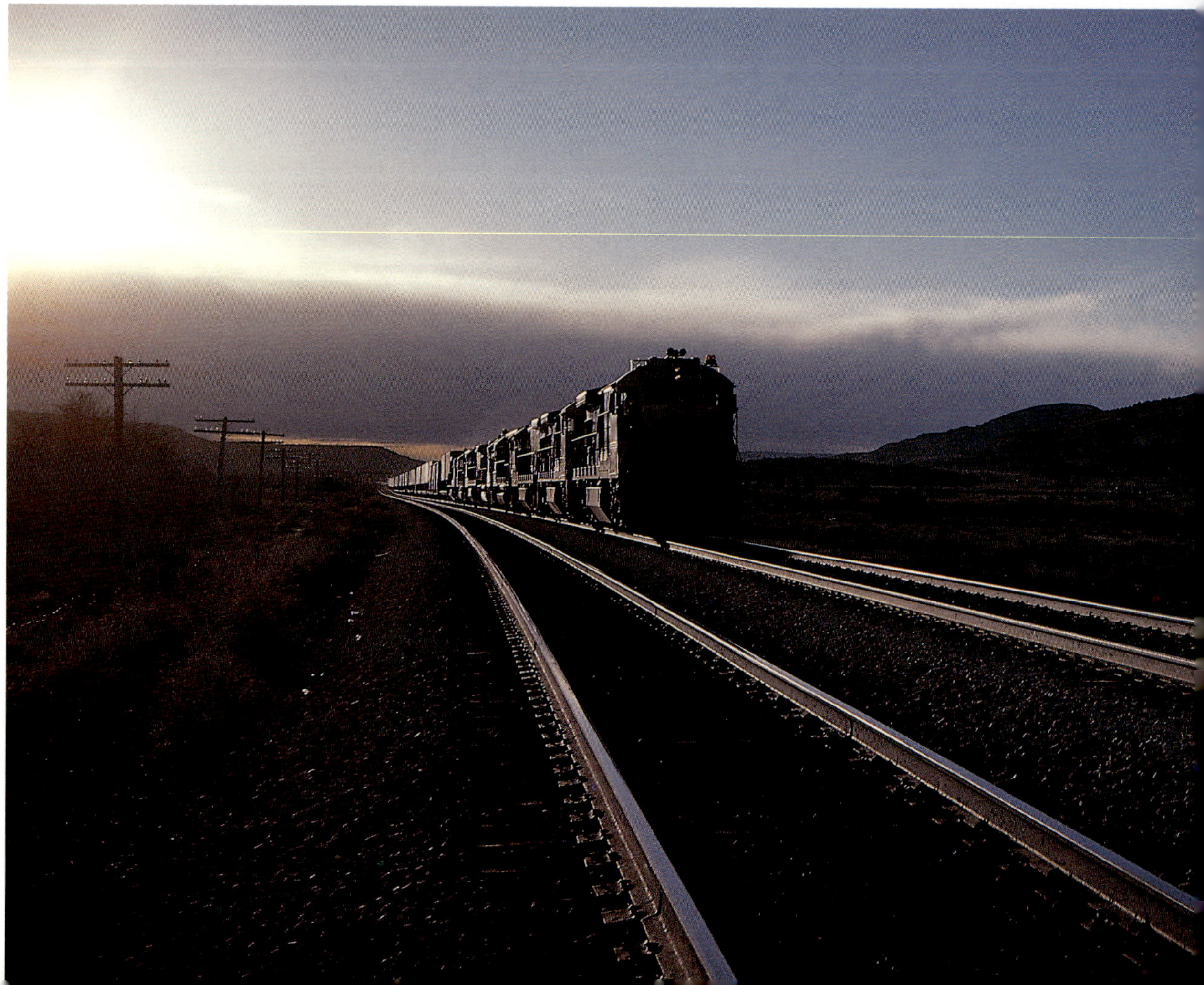

Warbonnets across the Southwest. ABOVE LEFT: At North Guam, New Mexico (also location of this book's cover photo), Santa Fe GE Dash 8-40B 7423 hurries a short Q-train — Q-LANY — east on July 25, 1988. This service is jointly operated by AT&SF and Conrail between Los Angeles and New York and primarily carries U. S. mail. Photo: Joe McMillan. LEFT: In western New Mexico, near Laguna, Santa Fe Extra 8127 East encounters dusk, March 21, 1987. Photo: Ronald Welch. ABOVE: Amtrak's eastbound *Southwest Chief* glides over 220-foot-deep Canyon Diablo, west of Winslow, Arizona, while an AT&SF freight stands ready to make its crossing, May 31, 1987. Photo: Alex Mayes.

snaking path over the Wasatch Mountains atop Soldier Summit. D&RGW, together with AT&SF, sponsored the bustling "Joint Line," a captivating stretch of railroad from Denver to Pueblo, laid against a backdrop of the Front Range, that in modern times became a freeway for the coal and manifest traffic of D&RGW, Santa Fe, and tenant BN. D&RGW spun across Tennessee Pass and through the Royal Gorge a route that allowed train-watchers the experience of watching a dozen or more units howling out of Minturn to lift coal up 3 percent grades and attain the highest mountain crossing of any U. S. Class 1 railroad.

Of course, tough railroading — battling mountains, carving through river gorges, threading across hostile desert country — is what much of Western

Santa Fe SD40-2 5034 leads an intermodal train through Chalender, Arizona, west of Flagstaff, December 28, 1986, with Arizona's San Francisco Peaks as a backdrop. Photo: Joe McMillan.

railroading is about. In the north, BN's ex-Great Northern main line clings to evergreen-blanketed rims to weave through Marias Pass and conquer the Montana Rockies; farther west, BN defeats the Cascades, spinning over Stevens Pass and ducking through 7-mile Cascade Tunnel to reach Seattle. To attain Portland, BN (and UP) huddle along the Columbia River.

Across the West, the examples are nearly endless:

To reach the Pacific Northwest UP twirls its steel rails through the Blue Mountains of Oregon and SP casts its Cascade and Siskiyou lines below pine and snow-covered peaks; UP's ex-Western Pacific main threads along the Feather River, SP's fabled Donner Pass line arcs over the Sierra Nevada, and SP and AT&SF jointly twist through the Tehachapi Mountains to bring tonnage to the Bay Area; in Wyoming, Union Pacific attains the Continental Divide with its

Born in 1986 from Southern Pacific's Hayden Branch in southeast Arizona, the Copper Basin Railway is appropriately named, hauling copper ore from mine to smelter, then making deliveries to SP at Magma. At Ray Junction, Arizona, Copper Basin GP18 204 and an ex-Kennecott Copper GP39 tow ore cars, January 16, 1988. Photo: Reid McNaught.

Sherman Hill crossing of the high plains; in Southern California, UP, SP, and Santa Fe all squeeze their trains through Cajon Pass; Santa Fe and Southern Pacific stretch steel across the remote, hostile deserts of Arizona and New Mexico; SP crosses (and UP skirts) Utah's menacing Great Salt Lake.

And as in every other region of this land, there is diversity beyond the Super Seven. While not as numerous as elsewhere in our country, regionals have taken hold in the West with the likes of Montana Rail Link and Washington Central; short lines such as the Utah Railway and Trona and Copper Basin Railway and McCloud River haul coal and chemicals and copper and lumber. Amtrak's great Superliner trains —

the *Southwest Chief* and *California Zephyr* and *Coast Starlight* and *Empire Builder* and *Sunset* —crisscross the broad West, and in densely populated California, railroading is accepting an ever-increasing role of modern people-mover, in the forms of San Francisco's CalTrans commuter operation and Amtrak's Los Angeles-San Diego push-pull corridor trains.

The West — just like all the marvelous regions of this land — draws the train-watcher with endless promises of new railroading discoveries, with the rewards of vivid, long-lasting memories. The West calls us to witness the glory and enduring drama of railroading, and for the train-watcher, there cannot be a much higher recommendation.

LEFT: With high water temporarily having closed Southern Pacific's own Lucin Cutoff across the Great Salt Lake, SP EMD SDs detour a westbound freight in April 1987 over UP's ex-Western Pacific main, which skirts the south rim of the lake. After heavy reconstruction, Southern Pacific's line was reopened in August 1987. BELOW LEFT: On a wintery January 1989 day, Utah Railway's big EMDs — ex-SP SD45s and ex-BN F45s — are positioned on the point and mid-train to lift coal over Utah's Wasatch Mountains, via Rio Grande's route over Soldier Summit. The Utah Railway hauls coal from mines on the eastern escarpment of the Wasatch Range to Provo, via its own rails and D&RGW trackage rights. BELOW: Westbound Rio Grande GP40s draw under the famed sandstone turrets of Castle Gate, deep in Price River Canyon west of Helper, Utah, May 31, 1982. Ahead awaits the climb over Soldier Summit. Three photos: Dave Gayer.

With the Front Range of the Colorado Rockies behind and the Wasatch Mountains ahead, Amtrak's westbound *California Zephyr* hurries along Rio Grande's crossing of the high desert of Utah at Thompson, July 7, 1988. Photo: Mike Danneman.

Rio Grande's famous Tennessee Pass line links Pueblo, Colorado (and Rio Grande's trackage rights via Union Pacific east toward Kansas City), with D&RGW's Denver-Ogden main line at Dotsero, Colorado. Boasting the highest mountain crossing of any U. S. Class 1 railroad, at 10,246 feet, the line also laces its rails through magnificent Royal Gorge. ABOVE: At Pando, Colorado, on the west slope of the pass, D&RGW GP40 3078 climbs toward the summit amid blazing autumn foliage. BELOW: Rio Grande and SP EMDs mix to power a westbound over Tennessee Pass at Mitchell, Colorado, September 27, 1985. Both photos: Steve Patterson.

PRECEDING PAGES: The inspiring marriage of big-time, modern railroading and the Rockies is revealed from high atop D&RGW Tunnel 17 at Crescent, Colorado, as Rio Grande EMD SD40T-2s snake empty coal hoppers westward. Photo: Steve Patterson.

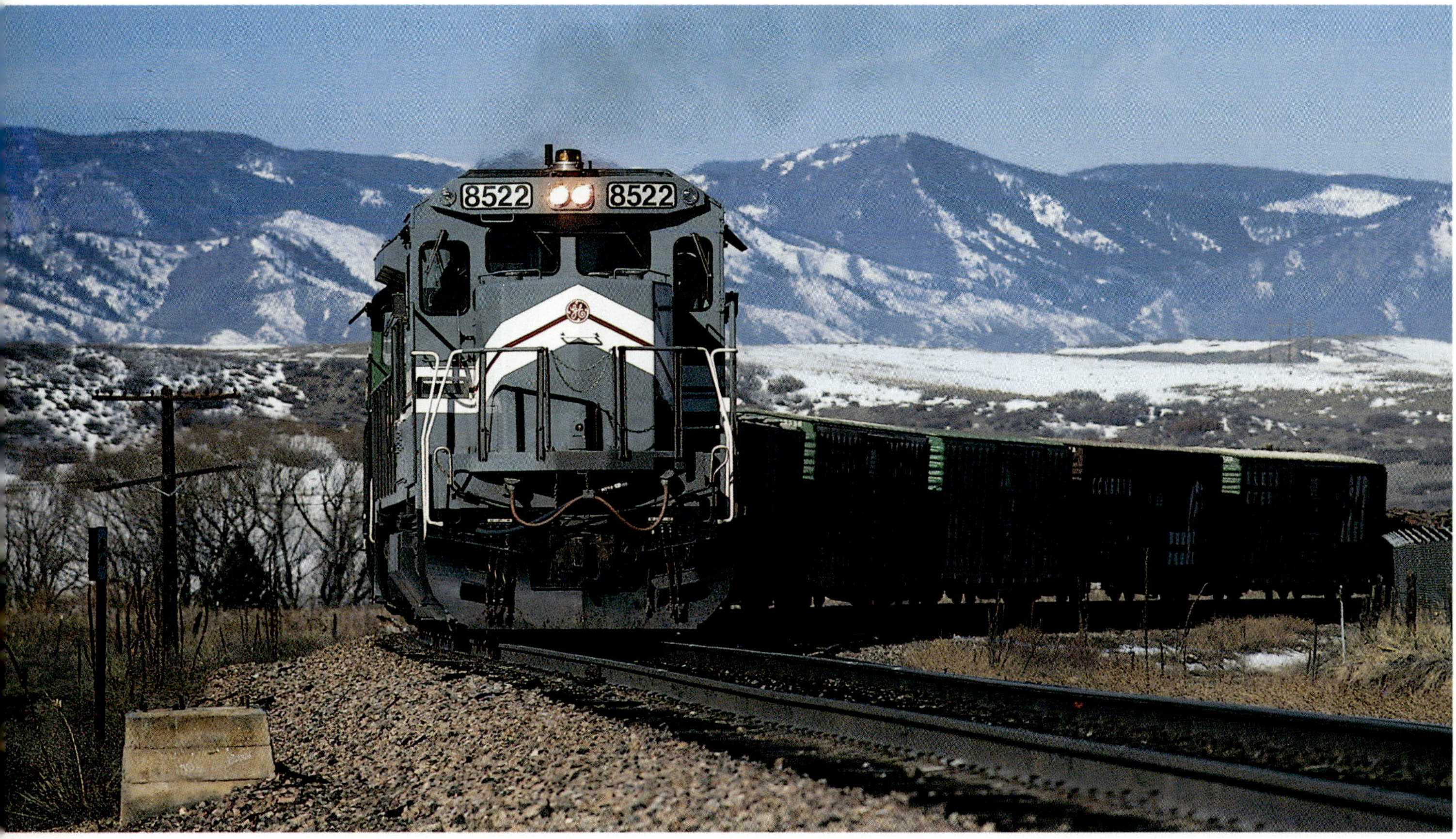

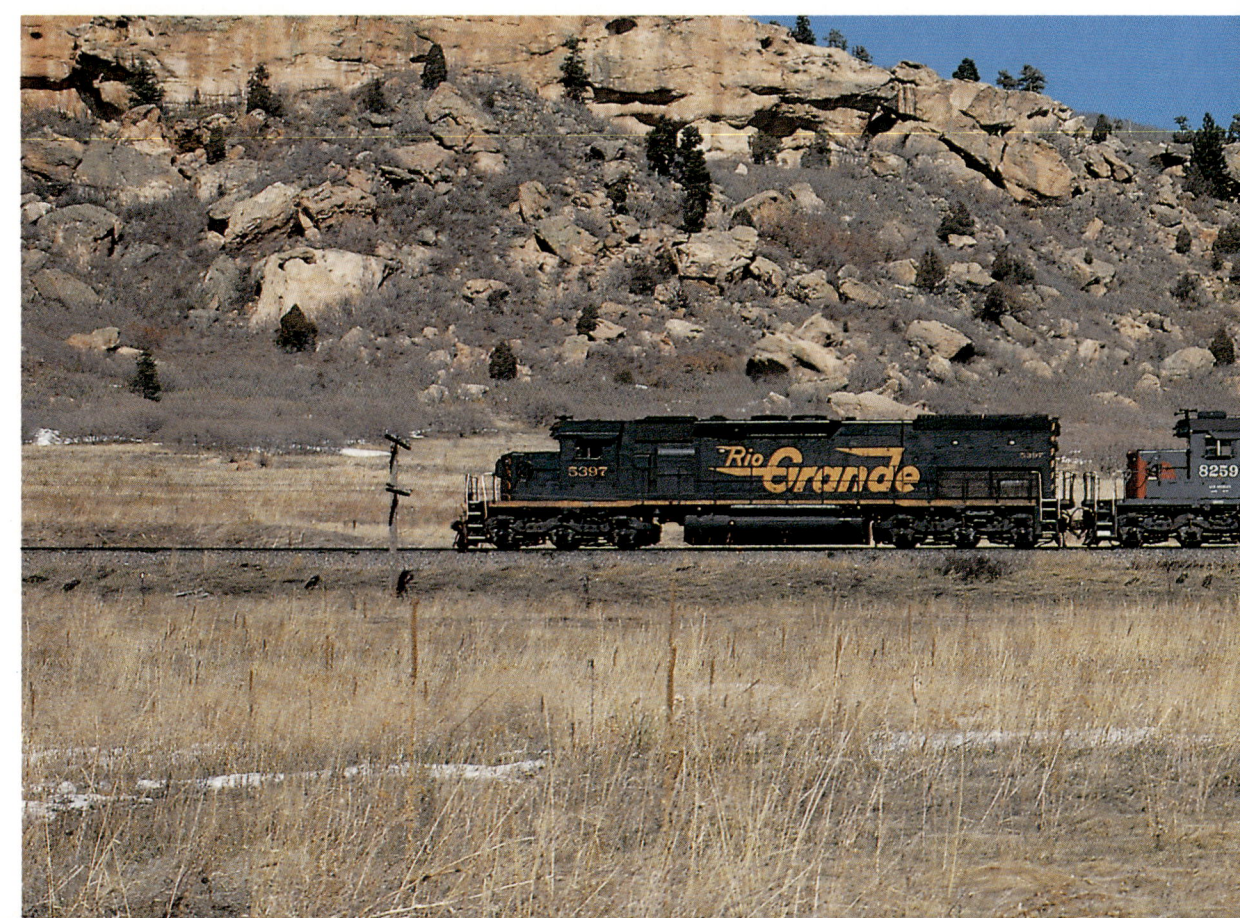

Between Denver and Pueblo, on Colorado's "Joint Line," the trains of Rio Grande, Santa Fe, and Burlington Northern all mix (D&RGW and AT&SF actually own the route). LEFT: At Sedalia, GE 8522 heads up BN tonnage. Like the Oakway EMD SD60s operated by BN, GEs such as this LMX B39-8 wear builder markings and are leased by BN. Photo: Mike Danneman. ABOVE: At Palmer Lake, June 23, 1988, Santa Fe Q-trains behind GP39-2s meet. Photo: Ron Flanary. BELOW: Two EMD SD40T-2s — one D&RGW and one SP — plus a Rio Grande GP40 cruise through Palmer Lake with a freight. Photo: Mike Danneman.

Big steam on Union Pacific: Along with Norfolk Southern, UP has been a primary advocate of Class 1 mainline steam excursions in the diesel age. RIGHT: In the roundhouse at Cheyenne, Wyoming, June 17, 1988, the stalwart of Union Pacific's steam program — 4-8-4 8444 — awaits her next call. After decades in black, the Alco-built 4-8-4 was painted in two-tone gray and yellow in 1987. Photo: Ron Flanary. ABOVE: Titan of UP's steam program is Challenger 3985, restored to service in 1981. On an October 20, 1984, Denver-Laramie excursion, the 4-6-6-4 completes a Christmas-card scene at Perkins, Wyoming, on Union Pacific's Harriman Cutoff over (or some would say around) Sherman Hill. Photo: Reid McNaught.

UP pushes two different alignments across the Laramie Mountains between Cheyenne and Laramie, Wyoming. ABOVE: At Dale, where UP's route via Sherman Hill's summit and the Harriman Cutoff converge, SD40-2 3391 and kin blacken the sky with exhaust as they drag a train east, July 5, 1988. RIGHT: Eastbound tonnage drawn by UP EMD DDA40X 6913 and Norfolk Southern power strides toward Sherman Hill's Hermosa Tunnel, July 1984. Built by EMD for UP in 1969-1971, the 47 6,600-horsepower DDA40Xs were the world's largest diesels; all were retired from regular service by 1985. BELOW: In western Wyoming, near Green River, UP SD40-2s hurry westward against the storm-dressed dusk sky of July 5, 1988. Three photos: Mike Danneman.

8032
8032
1905

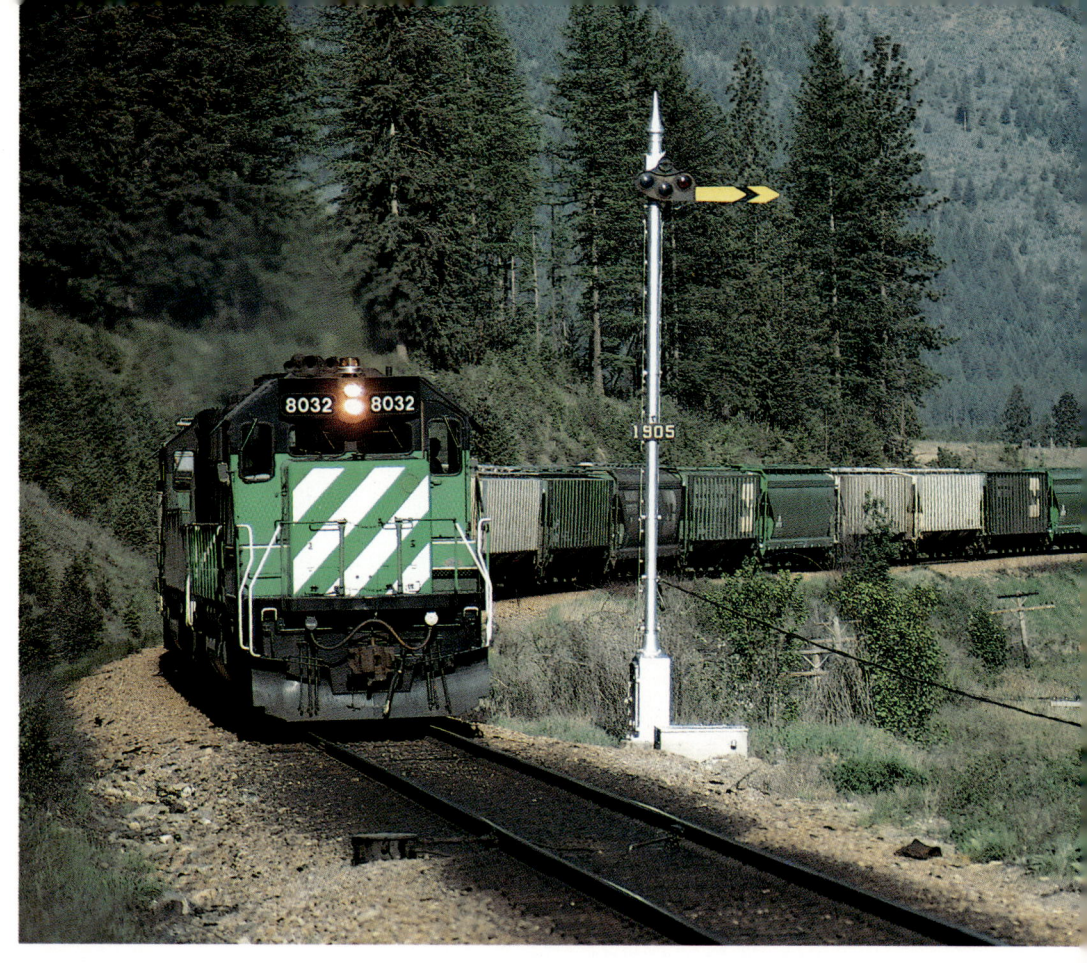

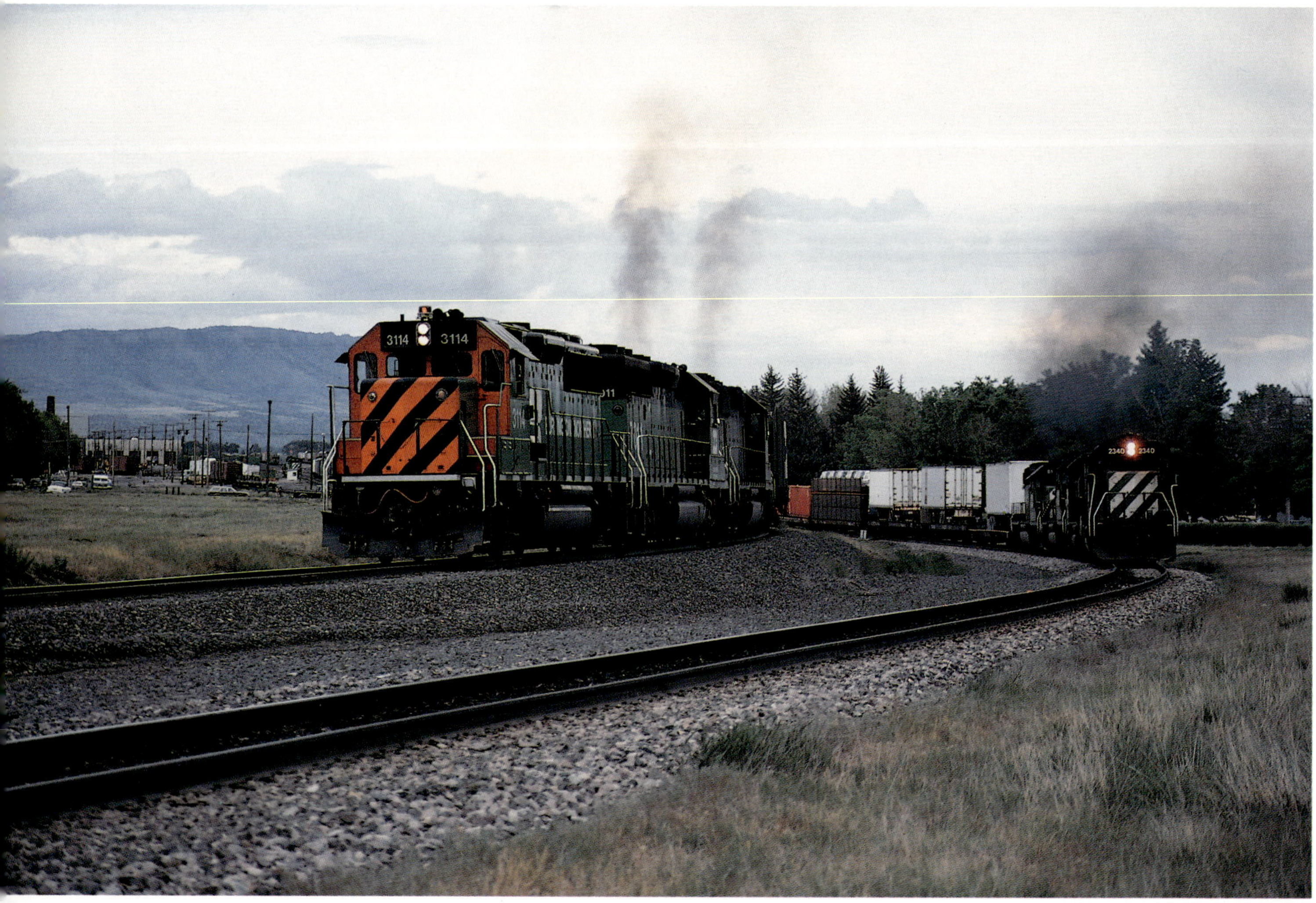
3114
3114
2340
2340

LEFT: Evolution. On what was once Northern Pacific, then Burlington Northern, and, since October 1987, regional Montana Rail Link, BN SD40-2 8032 sweeps eastward past a semaphore that recalls the route's NP origins. The date is May 20, 1988, the location west of Superior, Montana. In addition to its own business, Montana Rail Link continues to handle BN through trains. BELOW LEFT: At Livingston, Montana, twin westbounds prepare to battle Bozeman Pass, on the ex-NP main line. Livingston Shops, now used by Montana Rail Link, are in the background. Both photos: Dave Gayer.

ABOVE: In contrast to the old NP, the ex-Great Northern main across Montana remains pure BN territory. Atop Marias Pass in a swirling March 1988 blizzard, even the tiger-striped face of a BN GP50 heading east at Summit is veiled a ghostly white. Photo: Mike Danneman.

Montana Rockies magnificence: Amtrak's eastbound *Empire Builder* crosses Two Medicine Bridge at East Glacier, on the east slope of BN's Marias Pass, March 3, 1989. Photo: Mike Danneman.

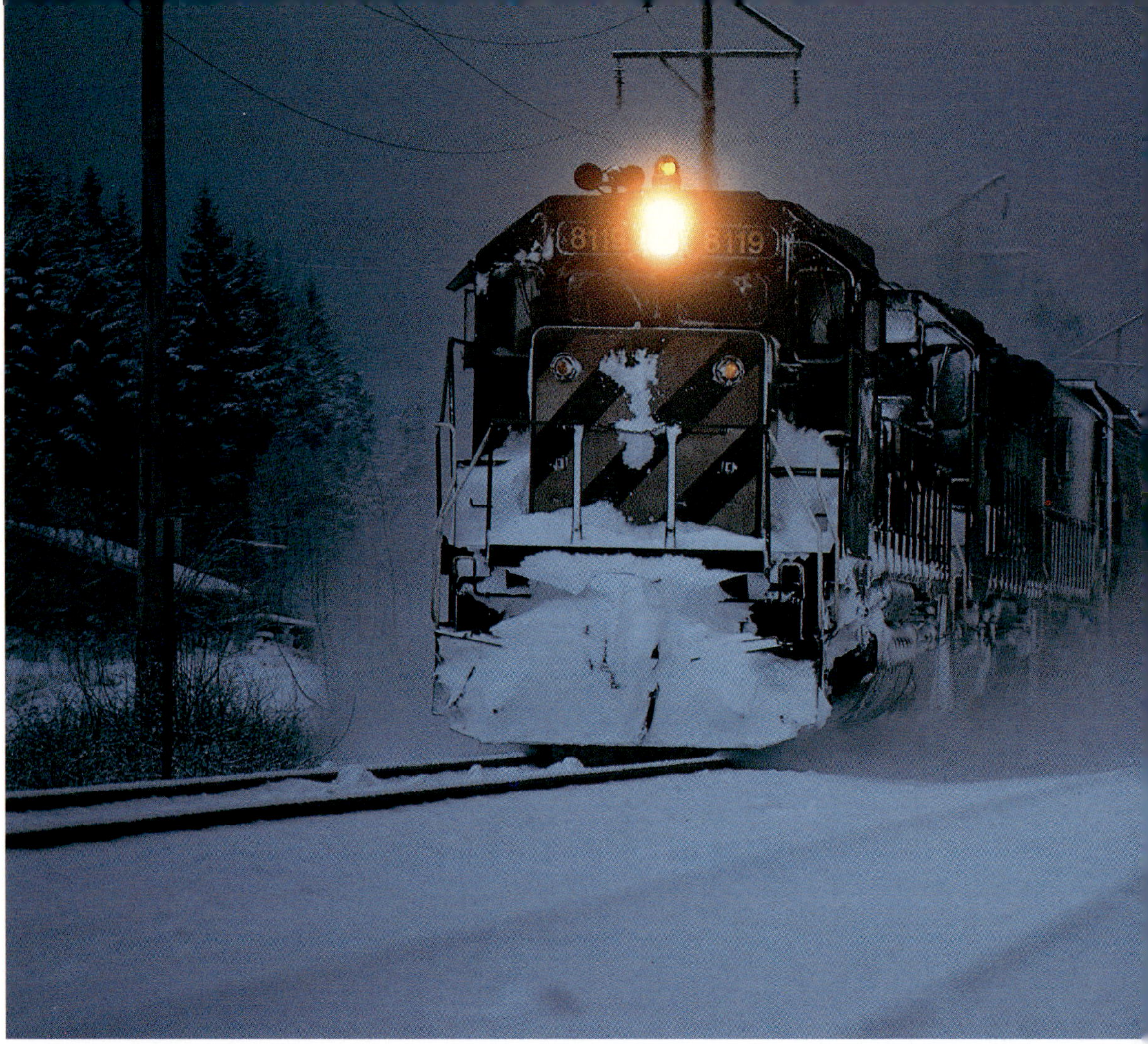
8119
8119

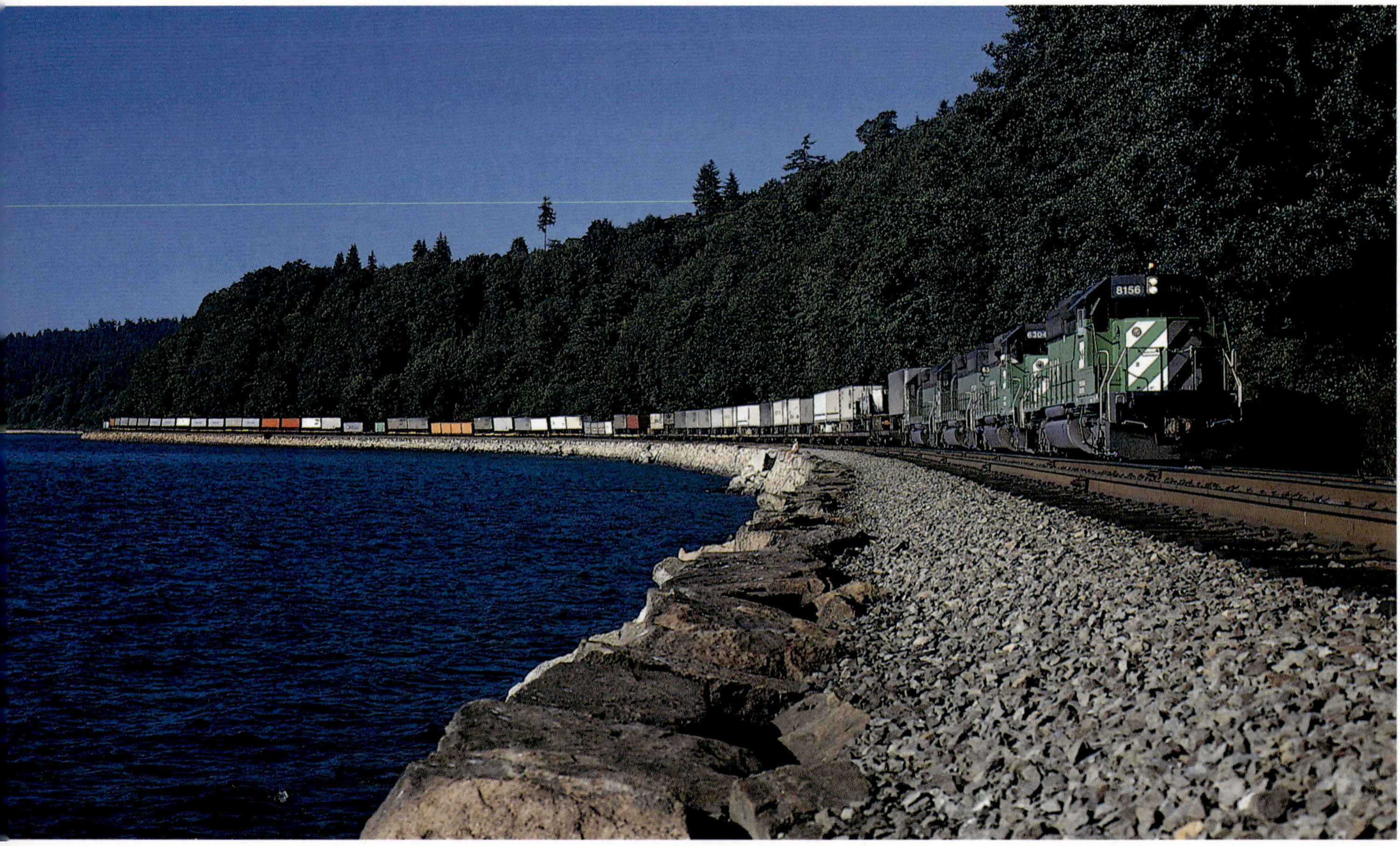
8156

Burlington Northern in Washington state. LEFT: Westbound BN SD40-2 8119 and sisters are pasted with wet snow on the stormy second day of 1982 at Gold Bar as they roll down the ex-Great Northern main from the summit of the Cascade Mountains. BELOW LEFT: Far more placid is the weather on a June 1980 afternoon as BN SDs curl an intermodal train along Puget Sound, following the ex-GN's path into Seattle. BELOW: On the old Spokane, Portland & Seattle west of Pasco, a BN intermodal train headed toward Spokane and points east hugs the north shore of the Columbia River, July 30, 1983. Three photos: Blair Kooistra.

ABOVE: On Union Pacific's route into the Pacific Northwest, UP SD40-2 3213 and a leased ex-BN SD tug grain hoppers east, June 11, 1988, near Cascade Locks, on the Oregon side of the Columbia River. Photo: Alex Mayes. BELOW: At Kamela, Oregon, the summit of UP's Blue Mountain grade, UP SD40-2 3507 leads a Portland-bound freight in December 1983. Photo: Blair Kooistra.

ABOVE: Low clouds swirl among the peaks of the Cascades as Southern Pacific EMD SDs twist across Salt Creek Trestle on SP's Cascade line north of Chemult, Oregon, June 4, 1988. Tonnage is bound for Portland. Photo: Alex Mayes. **BELOW:** Southern Pacific GS-4 4-8-4 4449 strides along the calm waters of Oregon's Lookout Point Reservoir on a March 1986 journey from its Portland home to Los Angeles to appear in the Disney film "Tough Guys." Photo: Tom Baldner.

ABOVE: On Union Pacific's ex-Western Pacific main line near Clifside, Nevada, a detouring Southern Pacific piggyback wraps itself around Arnold Loop, conquering the Toano Range on its voyage west in the summer of 1987. Photo: Blair Kooistra.

ABOVE: West of Carlin, Nevada, both SP and UP (ex-WP) thread their steel paths through Humboldt River Canyon. On July 22, 1988, at Palisade, Nevada, UP SD40-2s urge a Double Stack train west toward the Bay Area. BELOW: SP SD45M 7399 rolls east at Palisade, June 18, 1986. The red and yellow scheme worn by the big EMD was applied to many SP and Santa Fe units in anticipation of the two roads' merger. After the ICC refused the marriage, both AT&SF and SP returned to their traditional liveries. Both photos: Blair Kooistra.

At the most famous of old Western Pacific locations — Keddie, California — Union Pacific GE Dash 8-40C 9335, bound east through magnificent Feather River Canyon, bursts out of Tunnel 32 and onto the trestle that forms Keddie Wye, February 26, 1989. The line to the right is the UP/BN "Inside Gateway" north to Wishram, Washington, via Bieber, California. Photo: Mike Danneman.

ABOVE: Framed by the wooden snowshed complex at Norden, California, a westbound Southern Pacific freight has attained the 7,000-foot-high summit of legendary Donner Pass and will now begin its descent toward Sacramento. Despite the June 3, 1988 date, snow dusts the Sierra Nevadas. Photo: Alex Mayes. BELOW: At Soda Springs, Amtrak's *California Zephyr* drops down the west slope of Donner Pass, with its Oakland destination only 200 miles distant, February 26, 1988. Photo: Mike Danneman.

RIGHT: The location is SP's Sacramento (California) locomotive shop complex, but in spirit the scene represents edifices across this country — from Altoona, Pennsylvania, to San Bernardino, California — where skilled workmen tend the locomotives that keep America's trains rolling. Photo: Blair Kooistra.

LEFT: Riding high over Franklin Canyon at Muir, California, Santa Fe piggybacks string through the Bay Area behind an F45 and SD45-2, February 23, 1986. Terminus for AT&SF intermodal traffic in the Bay Area is nearby Richmond. Photo: Joe McMillan. ABOVE: Bright-faced CalTrans F40PHs slice past each other in San Francisco, August 18, 1986. F40PH 900 is outbound, while 905 is pushing an inbound. CalTrans (short for California Department of Transportation) operates trains on 47 miles of Southern Pacific trackage between San Francisco and San Jose. Photo: J. David Ingles.

Tehachapi! To push its rails between the Bay Area and the Mojave Desert, Southern Pacific built across the Tehachapi Mountains — between Bakersfield and Mojave, California — in 1875-76, and in 1899 a joint-trackage agreement was reached with Santa Fe. Today, the Tehachapi crossing is one of the busiest and most dramatic mountain crossings in America. LEFT: Santa Fe GP50 3848 heads tonnage downgrade at Bealville, February 28, 1988. Photo: Mike Danneman. ABOVE: Near Walong, Southern Pacific SD40R 7353 challenges the curling, demanding territory near Tehachapi Loop. Photo: Scott Hartley. BELOW: At the base of the Tehachapi Mountains at Mojave, SP diesels sleep away the night of February 28, 1988, orange trails of exhaust sparks eddying overhead. Photo: Mike Danneman.

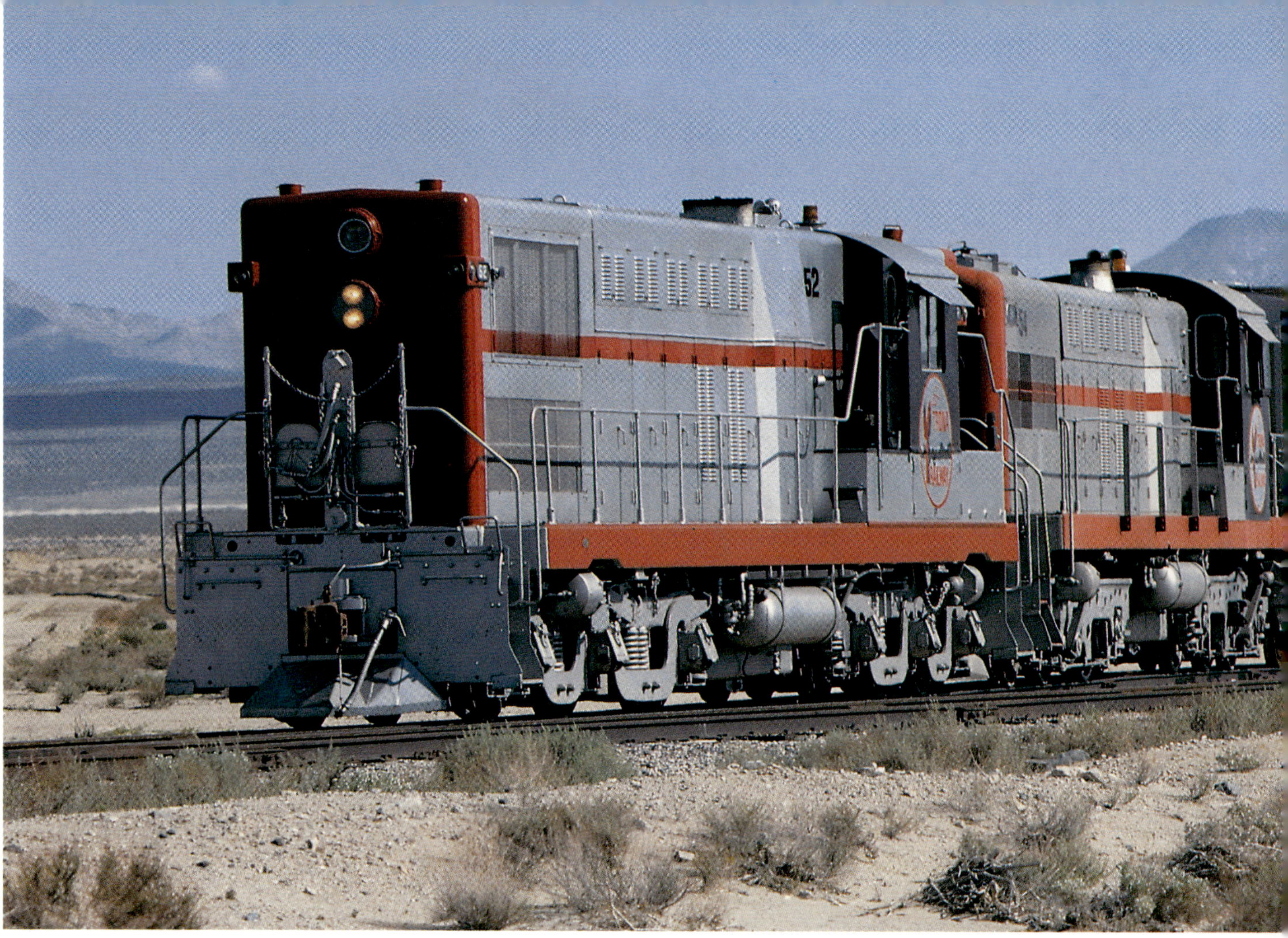
52

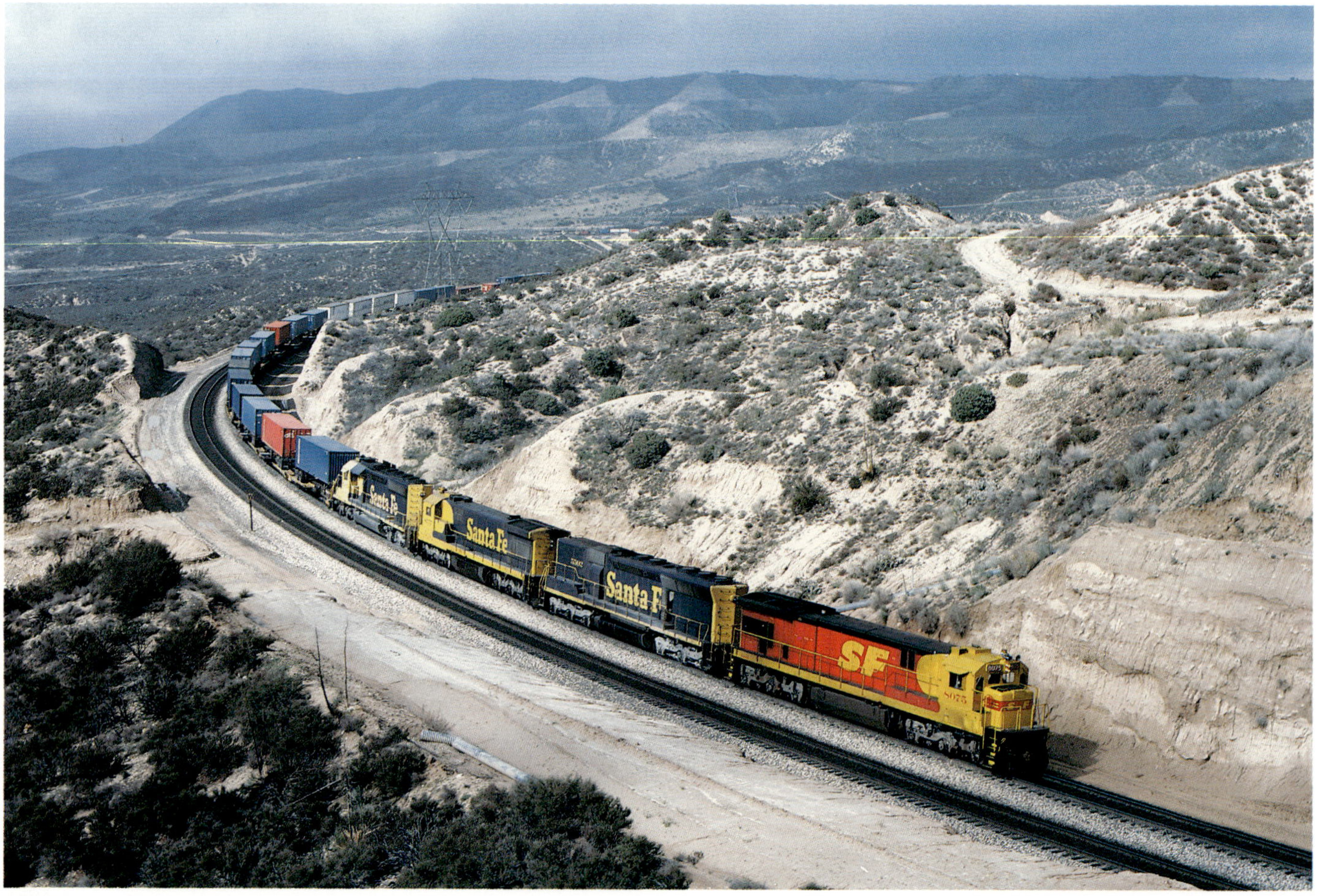
Santa Fe
Santa Fe
SF

LEFT: Few short lines are more renowned than California's Trona Railway, in no small part due to its longtime use of big Baldwin diesels. Two of Trona's three Baldwin AS616s switch cars loaded with borax at West End, California, April 18, 1988. Trona runs from its namesake town 31 miles to an SP connection at Searles. Photo: Scott Hartley.

BELOW LEFT: Like Tehachapi to the north, Southern California's Cajon Pass is a landmark of American railroading, in this case shared by Santa Fe and Union Pacific (with Southern Pacific also navigating the pass with its Colton-Palmdale Cutoff). In February 1986, a quartet of Santa Fe diesels led by GE C30-7 8075 has attained Cajon Summit on a journey out of San Bernardino toward Barstow and points east. Photo: Dave Gayer. **BELOW:** Between Cajon and Summit, a trio of UP GEs — two Dash 8-40Cs and a C30-7 — marches tonnage through the heart of the pass, November 20, 1988. Photo: George W. Hamlin.

Southern Pacific's Sunset Route begins its drive from Los Angeles to New Orleans by stretching through Beaumont Pass between Colton and Indio, California. At Ordway, Cotton Belt (SP) GE Dash 8-40B 8061 points through San Timoteo Canyon, January 7, 1989. Photo: George W. Hamlin.

On the busiest Amtrak corridor outside the East, with eight runs each way daily, push-pull Amtrak train 576 cruises along the Pacific on Santa Fe's Surf Line at San Clemente, California, bound from Los Angeles to San Diego, January 8, 1989. Photo: George W. Hamlin.

Offering a view of the Pacific Ocean as fine as any cruise ship, Amtrak's Los Angeles-Seattle *Coast Starlight* curls along SP's Coast Line near Gaviota, California, February 24, 1989. Photo: Mike Danneman.

ACKNOWLEDGMENTS

FIRST, foremost, this book is devoted to railroad photography. Therefore, our first thanks deservedly go to the photographers whose work and credit lines appear in this volume. Without their enthusiastic support, without the extraordinary camera work they provided, this book would not have been possible. Railroad photography can, at once, be both fulfilling, challenging, exciting, and yet frustrating and demanding. It is no simple chore to produce the photography our contributors amassed, and we thank them for their cooperation — and their skill.

In addition to the authors, the following photographers' work is represented in this volume: Scott Hartley, Alex Mayes, Joe McMillan, Blair Kooistra, Steve Glischinski, Steve Patterson, George Hamlin, Dave Gayer, John Murray, Ron Flanary, Reid McNaught, Paul Dalman, David Johnston, Bryan Rice, Ron Cady, Mike Small, Gary Rich, Ron Welch, Louis Saillard, J. David Ingles, Mark Danneman, Tom Danneman, J. Parker Lamb, Steven Cigolle, Jerry Mart, Tom Baldner and Rob Palmer.

We also wish to thank the people whose faith in this project saw it through from concept to completion. Thus, thanks go to our families, friends, and loved ones who supported us, advised us, and assisted us. In particular we'd like to mention Mark Danneman (Mike's brother) for assistance with design and layout, and Donnette Dolzall (Gary's wife) for manuscript editing.

North of Seattle, in the far northwest corner of this great land, fog off Puget Sound flirts with bright sunlight as a Burlington Northern freight begins a journey that will take it eastward across the Cascade Mountains and beyond — on steel rails across America. Photo: Blair Kooistra.

STEEL RAILS ACROSS AMERICA

Major routes—not all lines shown

ALY	Allegheny	**DME**	Dakota, Minnesota & Eastern	**MRL**	Montana Rail Link
AM	Arkansas & Missouri	**DMIR**	Duluth, Missabe & Iron Range	**MSRC**	MidSouth
AMTK	Amtrak	**DRGW**	Denver & Rio Grande Western	**MW**	Montana Western
ATSF	Atchison, Topeka & Santa Fe	**DWP**	Duluth, Winnipeg & Pacific	**NS**	Norfolk Southern
BAR	Bangor & Aroostook	**EJE**	Elgin, Joliet & Eastern	**NYSW**	New York, Susquehanna & Western
BLE	Bessemer & Lake Erie	**ELS**	Escanaba & Lake Superior	**PAL**	Paducah & Louisville
BN	Burlington Northern	**EUKA**	Eureka Southern	**PW**	Providence & Worcester
BP	Buffalo & Pittsburgh	**FEC**	Florida East Coast	**RFP**	Richmond, Fredericksburg & Potomac
CAGY	Columbus & Greenville	**FRVR**	Fox River Valley	**RRVW**	Red River Valley & Western
CC	Chicago, Central & Pacific	**GBW**	Green Bay & Western	**SOO**	Soo Line
CLC	Cadillac & Lake City	**GTI**	Guilford Transportation Industries	**SP**	Southern Pacific
CMNW	Chicago, Missouri & Western	**GTW**	Grand Trunk Western	**SSW**	St. Louis Southwestern
CNW	Chicago & North Western	**IAIS**	Iowa Interstate	**TM**	Texas Mexican
CP	Canadian Pacific	**IANR**	Iowa Northern	**TRA**	Trona
CR	Conrail	**IC**	Illinois Central	**TSBY**	Tuscola & Saginaw Bay
CSX	CSX Transportation	**INRD**	Indiana Rail Road	**UP**	Union Pacific
CV	Central Vermont	**KCS**	Kansas City Southern	**VTR**	Vermont
CVAR	Cedar Valley	**KRR**	Kiamichi	**WC**	Wisconsin Central
DAKS	Dakota Southern	**LI**	Long Island	**WCR**	Washington Central
DH	Delaware & Hudson	**LNW**	Louisiana & North West	**WICT**	Wisconsin & Calumet
DM	Detroit & Mackinac	**LSI**	Lake Superior & Ishpeming	**WSOR**	Wisconsin & Southern

Map: Mark Danneman and Mike Danneman